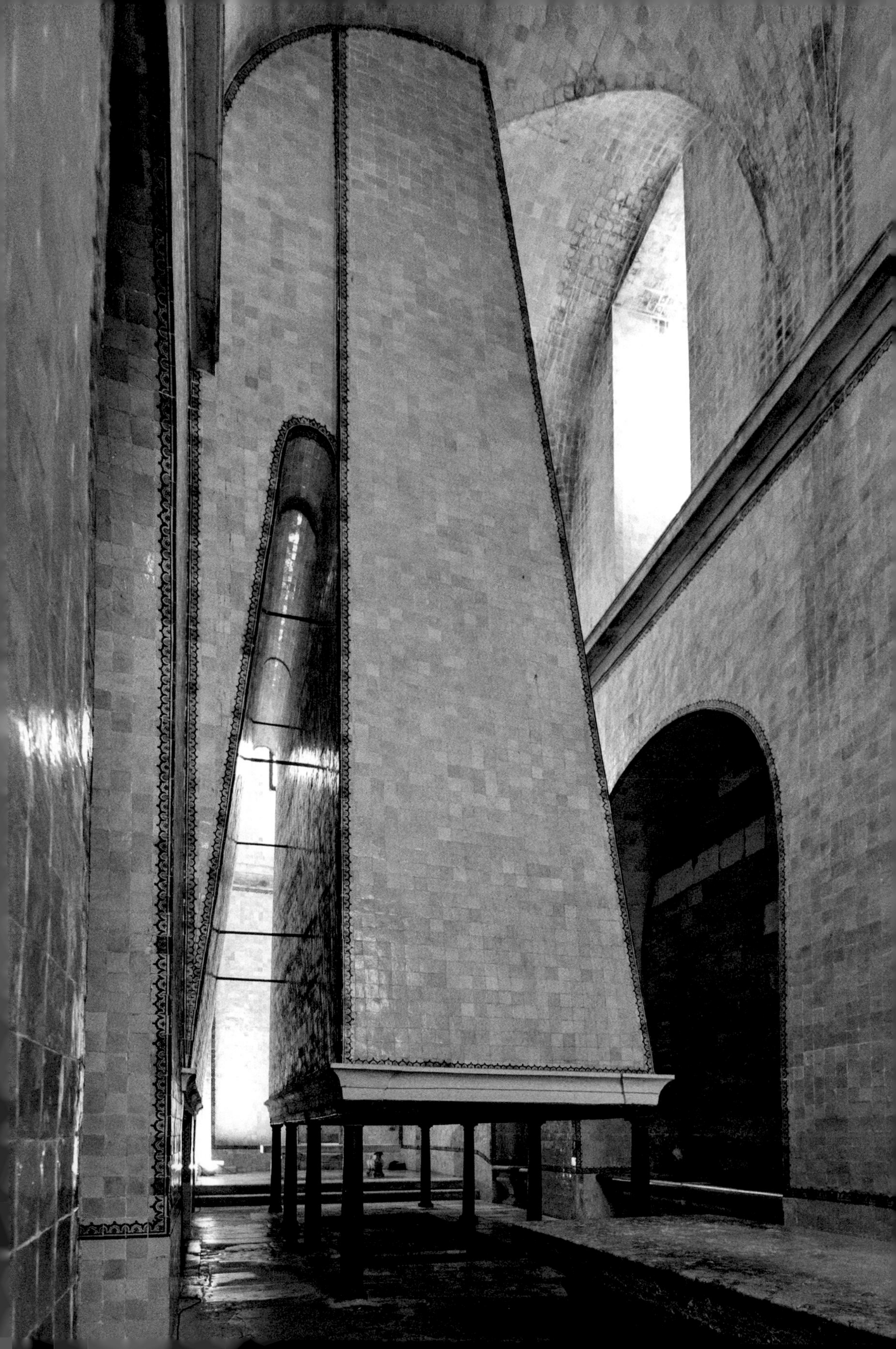

PRIVE
08683 31

Dedicating a number of *Archives* to Eduardo Souto de Moura seems like a complex challenge; his work is sufficiently well known and the topics that he addresses or is interested in are not usually hidden. One has the feeling that he knows what can be written about the ensemble of the architect and his work, but the truth is that not everything has been written or even intuited. It also seems that his work has been photographed abundantly, however *Archives* has to show that look differently via the images of Juan Rodríguez, and in the case of Eduardo Souto, this is not a look centred in a short space of time, rather a dilated one from someone who has already photographed a large number of his works and has accompanied him on his travels. The text grows in this number by adding the accurate look of Santiago de Molina, looking for the insight that facilitates the format chosen for *Archives*.

The quick and accurate drawings of Eduardo always have to accompany the explanation of his work, these are drawings he makes while summarizing each of his works with the greatest precision. Drawings of few minutes that seem to summarize many years of work and in addition to the drawings, there are also images of those anonymous works that he looks at carefully.

Pedro Cabrita Reis is the artist that has been chosen to accompany him in this edition of *Archives*, not only because of their intense personal relationship and many works in common, which undoubtedly helped with that selection, but also because of the way Pedro's look complements Eduardo's and vice versa, which should help to complete that broad view of Souto.

Pedro Cabrita also appears in the collection of 24 images without text that have been chosen by Souto. Cabrita is one of the twenty-four people who represent what Eduardo calls his "santinhos". Twenty-four people that make up a universe that interests him, and as opposed to making effort to explain the aspects of each one of them that have come to influence him, he prefers to use a simple picture to illustrate everything that we can imagine that he has been able to extract from their work or their principles.

Archives
Journal of Architecture
Issue 4. January 2019

Directors:
Carlos Quintáns
Juan Rodríguez

Editorial Board:
Francisco Mangado
Carlos Quintáns
Juan Rodríguez

Assistant editors:
Cibrán Rico López
Suso Vázquez Gómez

Publisher:
C2C Proyectos editoriales
de arquitectura S.L.

Edited and printed in
A Coruña, Galicia, Spain. 2019

Photography:
Juan Rodríguez

Texts:
Carlos Quintáns
Santiago de Molina

Thanks to:
Porto Academy
Sandra Bastos
Pedro Cabrita
Graça Correia
Joana Correa
Ana Fortuna
Nuno Graça Moura
Manuel Modia
Sarah Needham
Nuria Prieto
Juan Rguez. Bermúdez de Castro

Issue sponsored by:
Panoramah!
www.panoramah.com

The photographs of the works of Eduardo Souto de Moura for this issue of Archives were taken by Juan Rodríguez between January 2013 and February 2018

Photographs pp. 18-24-100-101 Luis Ferreira Alves / p. 18 Manuel Magalhães (FIG. 1) / p. 26 Marti Rabonna (FIG. 9) / pp. 73-74 Filipe Jorge

Editorial design:
desescribir

Design assistant:
Felipe Trillo

Translation:
Sarah Needham

Proofreading:
Patricia Buxán

Print run:
4.000

Printing:
Alva Gráfica

Binding:
Mudejar
Legatoria

Typeface:
FF Real

Papers:
Keaykolour Biscuit 300 g/m²
Symbol Tatami 115 g/m²
Coloraction Lagoon 80-160 g/m²

MIXTO
Papel procedente de fuentes responsables
FSC® C136339

ISBN 978-84-947678-5-2
ISSN 2530-7274
Dep. Leg. C 580-2017

Contact:
Web. www.archives-journal.com
Mail. info@archives-journal.com
Instagram: archivesarchitecture
Facebook: Archives

Advertising:
For advertising inquiries and information please contact the administration via email info@archives-journal.com

Subscriptions:
Archives is published two times a year. For subscriptions please contact the administration. You can subscribe by email info@archives-journal.com or at www.archives-journal.com. Prices are subject to change.

Distribution and Sales:
Single issues of Archives may be ordered online at www.archives-journal.com

Bookshops should contact:
Polígrafa
Web: www.poligrafa.com
Mail: sales@poligrafa.com
T.: +34 933 968 846

Archives 4
Souto de Moura

Passion and obstinacy

Carlos Quintáns

The work of Souto de Moura is well known. For many, his architecture is clearly recognizable and some think it is also predictable. However, the feeling of not being able to find the limits of his work nests in all those who look closely at the Braga stadium, the Paula Rego museum or, more recently, his work in Barrocal, to give a few examples. His architecture is a constant advance and review that is punctuated with exceptional moments.

His is a way of doing that leads him to revise and reformulate his own work. At the same time he does the same with the work of those he admires. He likes to explain how Thomas Bernhard always writes the same book and how he takes his time with the details, showing an obsessive thoroughness, how he advances one step and comes back to return to the same thing. We could consider that we are dealing with someone who formulates work procedures through which projects are made that, although they can be considered isolated, must be looked at together. I dare to propose a look at the works in their entirety, to present it as Herberto Helder did when he decided to gather together his complete poetic works, redoing them all in a single poem, "Ou o Poema Contínuo" ("Ou or Continuous Poem").

This look at the consistencies and variations in Eduardo's work might bring him closer to the jazz he enjoys so much and in which he likes to see himself accompanied by Miles Davis or Ahmad Jamal. It is curious that the first descriptions written about Ahmad speak of his conscious use of spaces and silences to underline the transits between relaxation and tension, characterized by a great economy of means and melodic and harmonically inventive lines. Coincidences or not, the truth is that Eduardo likes to search in other disciplines, especially literature and music, without forgetting cinema, painting or obviously sculpture. Search in which the return to the known takes precedence over the attempt to capture the novelty.

The search for work procedures appears continuously in his conversations; he is interested in Rainer Maria Rilke, Enrique Vila-Matas and Mario Vargas Llosa more because of this search rather than due to their works themselves. And, on that search he arrives at architecture when he talks about Aldo Rossi and his *Scientific Autobiography* or the *Architecture of the City* just like in the book *Architektur* by Donald Judd.

There are few changes in his selection of references. He is a tireless and obsessive reader, book buyer and permanent traveller.

His office within the studio contains the publications he uses, some books by Mies (his collection of different editions of Mies's publications is very large and not all here), the *Inquérito,* some other books about popular Portuguese architecture, and the pride with which all the editions of *Tectónica* preside over the space next to some other editions of another magazine.

Eduardo seldom writes and when he does he occupies a good part of his text with some literary reference, with the humility of someone who recognizes the perfection that others achieve as something unattainable. He feels comfortable talking while he draws very fast, with a vigorous stroke, those drawings that appear in his books and that should be understood as an accompaniment to his words. He also feels comfortable in interviews although as usual he replies: "Não tenho nada novo para lhe dizer. Eu digo sempre o mesmo".[1]

Eduardo Souto de Moura collects what he finds interesting and has an abundance of photographs, cuttings from magazines and newspapers, which he treasures with no other order than that of how closely related they are to a project that is being made (images of works by Le Corbusier, Tessenow, Schinkel or Grassi are placed next to an aircraft carrier, a bridge or a bunker). Once used or revised, these images are carefully saved. Some of those photographs or drawings that appear and disappear from the walls of his home or his studio became part of a book *Atlas de Parede. Imagens de Método* in which part of that task of selecting those images is shown. It is obvious to explain its proximity with other Atlas, especially that of Gerhard Richter and of course the *Mnemosyne,* by

1. "I don't have anything else to say. I always say the same thing."

Aby Warburg. In spite of that continuous task of image selection, Souto, for this edition Archives, preferred to choose twenty-four portraits of those "characters" that he has selected from throughout history and from the disciplines that he needs the most.

What has been selected by Eduardo in those 24 images without text that appear in this *Archives*, are his "santinhos" those people who, with their work, have really modified his way of seeing or thinking. Twenty-four portraits of writers, musicians, architects or sculptors. He wanted to give an equal weight to each of these disciplines.

Souto's is an interest in the procedure that is shown to an even greater extent in this strong relationship that he has with literature, and that not only helps him to know procedures that belong to the discipline of writing; but also, among other things, to understand the place where he lives and mostly builds. It is necessary to understand the territory where one lives. Portugal is a small country full of history, which through the seas sought an expansion that was born from a pragmatic vision, with aspects more quantitative than qualitative, to create a vast commercial network. This relationship between Portugal and the world was first theorized by Luís de Camões in *Os Lusiadas*, and marked the birth of "Adecuación" (Adaptation) as the Portuguese identity, an adaptation that Eduardo takes as his own.

Souto maintains that in Portuguese architecture there has always been a process of re-elaboration due to a gap within the great centres of thought. The poet Paul Claudel wrote "Portugal c'est un pays en voyage; de temps en temps il touche l'Europe".[2] This gap lead to a process of domestication of the avant-garde that came from the Renaissance and the Baroque, or later in the twentieth century was confirmed within architecture upon looking at the edges of the modern movement by Fernando Távora or Nuno Teotónio Pereira. Also when looking at Portuguese architecture it is necessary to understand the movement of the Portuguese House at the end of the nineteenth century, proposed as the formalization of the lexicon proposed by Raul Lino and later (after 1955) the realization of the *Inquérito à Arquitectura Popular in Portugal*, a set of books that contain an extensive base of documents to understand the architecture inherited from the tradition, and thus assess this process of adaptation, establishing adequately an ethical assessment of what was found.

2.
"Portugal is a country on a journey; from time to time it touches Europe."

Távora is the one who has managed to change the pace of Portuguese architecture, establishing a critical relationship with tradition, the everyday, and with who uses said architecture–in short with the life that contains it. That historical fit of Portuguese architecture with what happened outside its borders seems to have happened at the right time; although Eduardo thinks that while the houses and drylands that were preserved in the villages of the interior of Portugal were being drawn or photographed, it transpired that Claude Lévi-Strauss or Michel Foucault were writing, in other contexts, about much more interesting anthropological and sociological aspects. Eduardo also complains about a possibly repetitive and closed-minded interpretation of what was collected in the Enquerito, but he recognizes it as a necessary and fundamental piece that other countries have not been able to formulate and for these countries, today it is now impossible to develop it, due to the disappearance of much of the traditional architecture that the "McDonaldization" of the planet has been demolishing. When looking at the *Inquérito*, Souto also looked at *A Casa Portuguesa* (1929) by Raul Lino in a brief reading that allowed for that hybridization of using known forms that he proposes.

The *Inquérito* is an effort of analysis and of generosity, in the same way that the political involvement of the Portuguese architects after the Carnation Revolution is also relevant. From outside, it seems that Portuguese architecture has managed to move in a more coordinated way than in other places, and that the current situation is due to this.

For Portugal (I would dare to say that for architecture) the friendship and complicity between three architects: Távora, Siza and Souto, who ended up sharing works and even a building for their studios, has been very important. This wonderful rarity speaks of how far their behaviours are from the usual confrontations between architects. I think that a good part of the mood of Portuguese architecture is due to the transmission and scope of this happy circumstance. I can only think of comparing this situation with the architects Alejandro de la Sota, José Antonio Corrales, Ramón Vázquez Molezún and José María García de Paredes. A few steps separate all of them in Calle Bretón de los Herreros in Madrid; they have a good relationship and collaborate in some projects, and soon the vitality of the architecture that arose there must also be revised.

A search for what's next and what's universal, with that idea of *critical internationalism* as Jean-Louis Cohen puts it. When Souto carried out the Braga market project and the intervention in a small ruin in Gêres (1980) he was already aware that it was not possible to find a pure culture or language, that a transitional stage was taking place. A year later, in 1981, he won the competition for the Casa das Artes in Porto and everything began to accelerate.

The projects of these first years mark the appearance of many of the elements that would later define the architecture of Souto. Many of his works are homes. Houses that constitute a laboratory in which solutions are outlined.

FIG.1
Ruin in Gêres, Portugal.
1980

FIG.2
House in Baião, Vale da Cerdeira, Lugar de Porto Manso, Portugal.
1990–1993

FIG.3
House in Moledo, Caminha, Portugal.
1991–1998

> There are architects who spend their lives always designing the same house. There are architects who spend their lives waiting for the same client: themselves.
>
> From "my" first project, I have continued to design the same house, as if it were an obsession. Although equal, they are all different, because the places and the people deserve it.
>
> I always start doing the project of the same house, for the same person, but with different pseudonyms, and if possible, as Aldo Rossi says, 'without ever getting distracted by people or houses that seem useless to me, and considering that progress in art and in science depends on this continuity and consistency, the only things that allow change'.[3]

3. Eduardo Souto de Moura. 7th March 1989

Souto understands that he has to write about the house, that he has to formulate what he has been able to propose, test and verify throughout his work.

In the year 1980 a tiny project for the reconversion of a ruin in Gerês (FIG.1) became the beginning of Souto's construction activity. This first work was a kind of refuge where everything seemed to coincide to arrive at a precise project that was absolutely necessary to start the work of Eduardo Souto de Moura. A refuge in an existing ruin, with space to be, sleep, a minimal bathroom and a kitchen bar. All the walls were preserved except the area that was occupied with a large window. What disappeared, or what was in no condition to remain, has been replaced by new elements, completely unrelated to what existed there. A concrete slab to make the roof and another for the floor. The ruin seems to have been undone on all sides and after that comes the glass–accurate and precise.

Apollinaire wrote that one must: "Préparer au lierre et au temps une ruine plus belle que les autres..."[4] in a work about ruin as a state of balance between nature and the artefact. A project that in short, seeks naturalness. A tiny work that seemed to predict the desires that Souto would later pursue in numerous projects.

4. "Prepare with ivy and time a ruin more beautiful than the others..."

From this first work and as he develops his work he maintains the nostalgic need to preserve the memory of the place, the physical support on which he builds. A search that leads to the generation of artificial contexts, false ruins and in general terms the creation of new lines of continuity. Artificial ruins like the ones he made in house 2 in Nevogilde after spending time drawing in Rome.

The house in Baião (FIG.2) is a later project, it conserved the ruin as a garden and the house was built next to it, appearing clearly defined and separate from the garden, as an object of contemplation. The house was embedded in the land, with a single fully glazed façade.

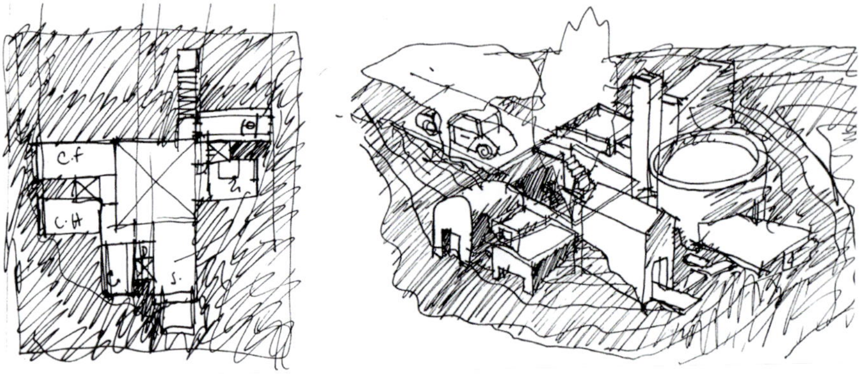

FIG.4
Drawing of the House in the Sierra de Arrábida, Portugal. 1994–2002

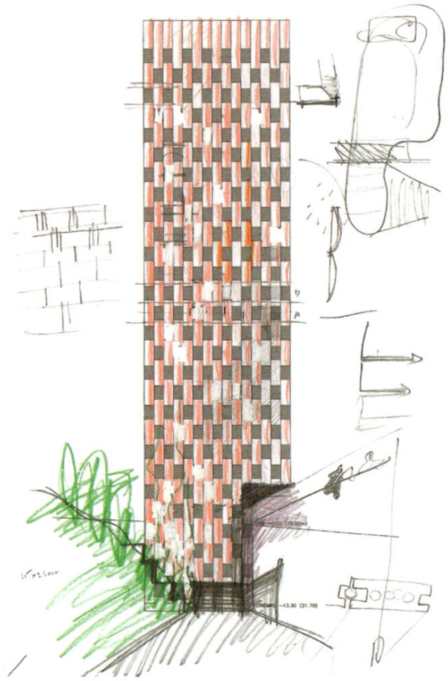

FIG.5
Drawing of Complejo La Pallaresa, Santa Coloma de Gramenet. Barcelona, Spain. 2011

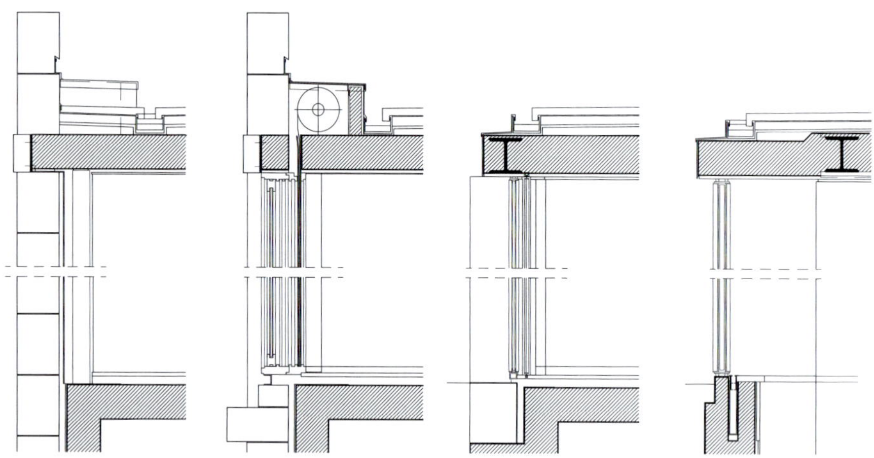

FIG.6
House 2 in Nevogilde. Porto, Portugal. 1983–1988

In the house in Moledo (FIG.3), the needs program consisted of a conventional list of rooms and yet the place was very demanding: a large extension of a steep hillside overlooking the Atlantic, grounded by agricultural terraces of an approximate height of 1.5 m. Redoing the platform with stone walls to prepare a favourable ground was the decision that determined what whole project would look like and the house is but a minor player in a very powerful ensemble topographically speaking, but that multiplies its relevance when adding to the force of a great extension of walls.

As James S. Ackerman put it, the history of Western architecture has been interpreted "between classic purist and irregular pictorial modes" and explained that this battle could be seen perfectly in what was has become known as a "villa" which is a house in a midpoint between urban and rural housing. The tension pointed out by Ackerman can thus be illustrated by the direction that Souto de Moura's work has followed. It would seem that the classicism of the Miesian road, which the house in Moledo crystallizes, is gradually taken over by a plastic torsion, potentially picturesque and ideologically non-believing...

This change can be visualized in the Casa do Cinema, but it takes shape in the house in the Sierra de Arrábida (FIG.4). Souto in this project tells us how after four years he overcame the "permanent crisis" and the personal difficulties he had in defining his own architectural language. The problem was that none of the experience gained prior to this project was suitable–it was not compatible neither with the client, nor with the topography, nor "with himself".

> In the face of increasing complexity, we need more than ever a simplifying thought, but one that is not mutilating: when reality resists simplification, we have to return to complexity, complexity is the invasion of the disorder of randomness and the uncertainty in reality... Today we all know that the future is uncertain, given the perpetual intervention of novelty and the unforeseen, which is why extreme complexity tends to resemble a permanent crisis.[5]

5. From the report about the house in Arrábida.

The transition between classic purist and irregular pictorial modes seems, in the case of Eduardo, not to be due to changes as a result of personal development, rather we could be speak of an intertwining of situations he has found himself in where he has solved projects that have modified or reformulated past proposals.

Souto generally made one-storey houses, precisely adapted to the terrain and its limits–which in Portugal are always marked by walls that have great presence, and this has been done in an exceptional way in the terraces of the Douro or in the stone walls that separate the wineries in

Vila Nova de Gaia. Walls that in the work of Souto participate with the house and this led him to work with patios of one form or another: in the houses of Matosinhos, or those of Pasteleira...

Long walls that reveal their interiors at the corners, with the glazed surfaces which are concentrated and generous in their dimensions. The windows in Souto's first projects did not exist as such, they only worked with the differentiation between 'positive' and 'negative': wall and glass. He did not need to compose the windows. The closed or open areas appeared naturally. From the house in Tavira the window and its composition appears until we arrive at projects only of windows like those of the ensemble at Santa Coloma de Gramenet (FIG.5).

In addition to the houses, some other project have been started from scratch. In A Casa das Artes (House of Arts) Souto's method is clearly shown in the organization of the program and attention to detail in order to disguise elements that disturb the search for abstraction: blinds, carpentry... This work that has begun, has a broad journey in time and in projects, and it is developed during the project to arrive only at what is essential. This search is transmitted magnificently through poetry. Souto always finds a moment to refer to the poems of Herberto Helder, a hidden poet, reluctant to be known and recognized and who has barely been translated into other languages because of his insurmountable modesty.

> Qualquer poema é um filme, e o único elemento que importa é o tempo, e o espaço é a metáfora do tempo, e o que se narra é a ressurreição do instante exatamente anterior à morte, a fulgurante agonia de um nervo que irrompe do poema e faz saltar a vida dentro da massa irreal do mundo. [...] A poesia propõe a história do mundo. Temos então o filme, o tempo[6]

If we go back to the reconversion of the ruin in Gerês, we can carefully observe the drawings of the plant and sections of the project, starting with that constant work in the definition of how to build. The position of the carpentry has been anticipated with regards to the structure, superimposed on the plan of the upper slab. However, the finally executed solution contains the carpentry between the floor plan and the floor. This is a game that has been designed by sometimes hiding the plane of the structure with glass and in other cases seeking the evidence of the structure in a clear way. The relationship between glazed surfaces and structures has alternated between works and even during them; as happened in house 2 in Nevogilde (FIG.6) where we find

6. "Any poem is a movie, and the only thing that matters is the time, and space is the metaphor of time, and what is narrated is the resurrection of the instant just prior to death, the flashing agony of a nerve erupting from the poem and makes life jump within the unreal mass of the world. [...] Poetry proposes the history of the world. So we have the movie, the time." (My translation. Source: Herberto Helder, Photomaton & Vox, Assírio & Alvim, Lisboa, 2006. p. 140.)

numerous solutions of what can happen with glazed areas and their relationship with what surrounds them.

In continuity with several houses, the Miguel Torga space is a project from the year 2007 that continues Souto's previous research during housing projects or that of the Casa das Artes. It is defined by walls that define the interior space and expand beyond what is covered to close the lot. Large slabs of vertical shale have been placed like they are the closures of some farms to form a powerful image which shows the magnitude of their thickness in the cuts of the walls. The holes appear only in the necessary points, hiding structures and false ceilings.

Glass allows for overlaying, for reflection, for transparency, for the breaking down of limits, for showing evidence of thickness or to conceal it; processes that appear in organised way in Souto's projects, as if he did not want to abandon them.

In the game of reflection and transparency there is a special project, the one of the pavilion of Portugal in the 11th Venice Biennale in the year 2008 (FIG.7). A totally glazed façade, with glass that acts like a mirror, reflecting the life that happens in the great canal and the buildings opposite. A project made together with Ângelo de Sousa and that stands out with regard to the real size of the warehouse on which they performed their work until it reached the height of the neighbouring house. It was a project designed by someone who knows Venturi and Dan Graham.

In Souto's work there is an insistence on the concealment of certain realities, especially of horizontal structures, and usually motivated by the pursuit of a longed for lightness and elegance. The fixtures to show or hide are developed according to the projects and they are placed in that area of contact between the outside and the inside. Dividing the project into sections is a clear tool with which to discover the nuances that can be perceived from the outside. The section starting from that initial point becomes uniform with few options to accompany the size of the building. The Paula Rego is one of the few projects in which the parallelism between the floor plan and the roof is broken, with the appearance of those large chimneys and it is surprising that in the multipurpose sports facility in Viana do Castelo Souto has chosen not to hide the structure.

His defense of beauty is very clear since it ensures that the image or the form has priority over the content. He questions the need for truth in architecture in the face of the tricks used to achieve beauty and in this analysis of what he does in his works, he searches for support in philosophy and literature: *The story of the lie* by Jacques Derrida, *The lie* by St. Augustine or *On the decadence of the art of lying* by Mark Twain.

FIG.7
Pavilion of Portugal in the 11th Venice Biennale of Architecture. 2008

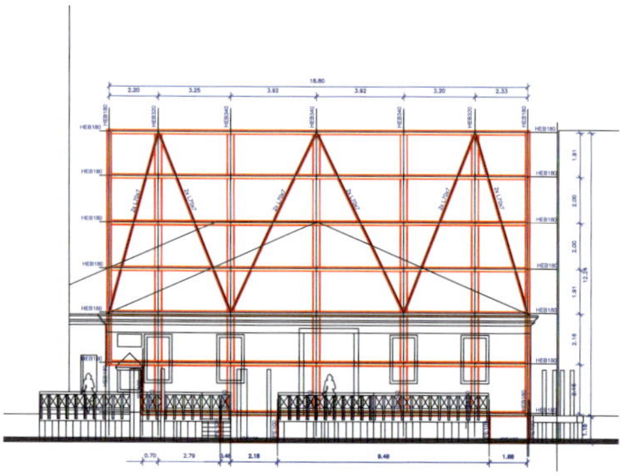

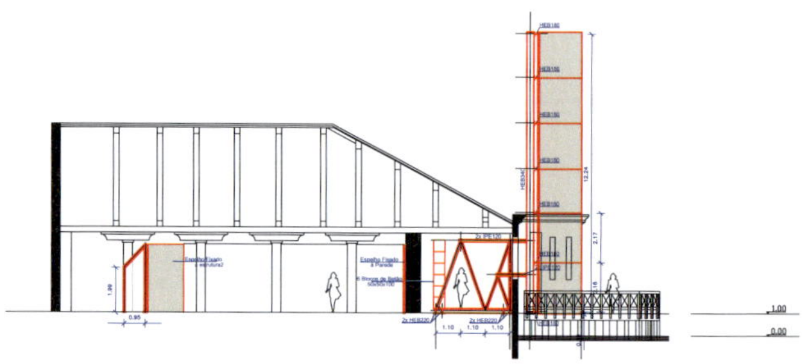

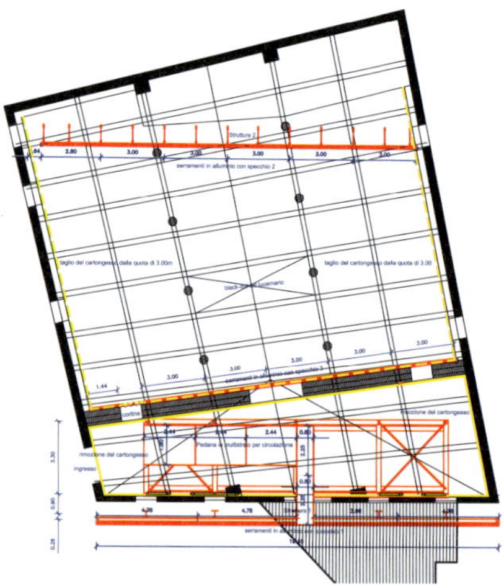

His projects do not hide the creation of this necessary "lie". What worries him is creating a system that looks authentic. Achieving a coherence that can be built he is interested less in authenticity itself.

However, his bridges and stairs lack tricks, instead they are clear and direct, not hiding the parts or the elements that he has used. The dell'Accademia Bridge project that he carried out for the contest organized by the Venice Biennale in 1985, or that of the bridge over Av. 24 de Julho in Lisbon... as well as any other set of his stairs, present a high degree of precision (think of the early staircase of the Casa das Artes or the recent one of the auditorium of Portalegre 2009). A staircase, although not his own, became the protagonist of the project of the pavilion for the Milan Triennial in 2016 (FIG.9). Souto built a large box to transport works of art, ready to receive the piece by artist Jannis Kounellis (the staircase). A box with reinforcements from the outside, and without joints and with the colour that the artist chose to highlight the piece on the inside.

He endorses a phrase of Rafael Moneo: "In the project, at the beginning, all decisions are arbitrary. Our obligation is to give a sense to this arbitrariness". And Souto adds that the most important thing is consistency in the process, in the development of each project. The problem is that the simpler one shows a image, the more torturous its construction its been. The more complex the result, the more the design has been neglected. The exact point is in the vigil, in the periodic mutation, just like the seasons of the year.

The reality in which we are immersed, the reality of architecture, rejects simplicity, and argues that complexity must be confronted. That complexity that ties together one's projects.

The references to the scale are obvious and he handles them well. His buildings find that appropriate scale.

A certain irony appears in his projects: in some of them very clearly: the two houses in Ponte da Lima. Two houses, and a single program: one is settled stuck to the ground and the other taking off from the ground, almost floating; two houses that have no meaning when separated and that can only be understood together.

Later another set of two houses, this time in the Douro (2004), obey different games, one is the crossing of two prismatic volumes that have been rotated ninety degrees and which have been based on the communications core, and the other is an inverted house that has been completely rotated so that what would be equivalent to the roof is what rests on the ground.

These are turns that also happen with respect to the ground plan, and thus the insistence on the rotated cubes, which serve for the project of

FIG.8
Casa das Artes. Porto, Portugal. 1980

FIG.9
Pavilion for the Milan Triennial. 2016

the Church of Mercy (1998) and for the café "do Eixo Deportivo Braga" (1983).

Specific games such as the exaggeration of the machine in the multi-purpose pavilion of Viana do Castelo (p. 150) or the uncomplicated look of a bunker for the Portalegre auditorium (p. 104).

Few are the architects who have to intervene on their past projects. In the case of Souto this circumstance is double, on the one hand, the Braga Market, which after its partial demolition (in which part of its ruins are exhibited) came to be configured into a new cultural space which changed it significantly with regard to the original project. On the other hand the house in Quinta do Lago (1984) also required an intervention with the arrival of a new owner who needed to increase its surface. Souto's project for this house consisted of a process in which the whole house was stretched to achieve this desired increase in surface, resulting in a greater lightness in the structure.

Ironies that arrive until the present moment, when in A Caida he lined an existing, neglected construction, made with brick, without finishing it. He did this with even more brick, but placed it with as much precision as possible.

A Caida presented a unified proposal of what was found (with the exception of a separate construction of the main ensemble). This unification was achieved with the application of a protective layer to all enclosures. This process, that of A Caida, was similar to that of the reconversion of the Bernardas Convent (p. 46) where that protective layer unified the exterior image of very altered walls before and during the work.

Finally, the Burgo Tower project, an office building on the Boavista-Burgo avenue that was paralysed in the crisis of the nineties and was not built until 2007. From the initial image, taken as a reference, of a stack of common construction materials which later became the building, and the model of the building, which became a home bar unit.

One of the best known works of Eduardo Souto is the intervention in the monastery of Santa María de Bouro. A project that wanted to preserve the aspect of ruin in the monastery that he knew from his stays there as a child. That ruin may have come from the reading of Ruskin, compared to an interpretation closer to Viollet le Duc of recent years. In recent projects (especially in A Caida) Souto tries to recompose an imagined reality, which had not happened before he intervened.

In the year 2000, Souto began to work on the reconversion of the Sanatório dos Ferroviários in Covilha, a building from 1944 that had been degraded into a ruin: The project of transforming these ruins into a hotel and spa led him to consolidate the elements that were conserved to achieve, again, the same environment that the building had before and to avoid generating in those who see it a sense of strangeness with traces of a different time to its original creation. In the Sanatório dos Ferroviários, a containment exercise was developed to avoid interference with the original project.

A few years later, in 2008, the project began to turn São Lourenço do Barrocal into a tourist complex. An extremely respectful intervention that above all has prioritized the preservation of an exceptional building complex. Faced with the usual approaches to the conservation of buildings for cultural content, the approach at Barrocal was to be aware that the only way to preserve heritage is to live with it and use it, even if it is damaged in some places.

The operation of Barrocal as a hotel is precise and exact, and one seems to be feel at ease when there, there is no shrillness and dissonance. Something similar happened in the interventions carried out on public spaces in Valença (2003). In Valença it is difficult to find Eduardo's hand, it seems to have been done by an agile and intelligent hand and one can appreciate this disappearance of the author in such a characteristic urban nucleus.

It is the project of A Caida that is still unfinished at this time in which Eduardo flourishes most in terms of reconfiguring what was found to achieve a unified ensemble. With very clear references to anonymous architecture and more specifically to what is only a few kilometres away, A Caida is a kind of research into which kind of architecture is being entered into at this moment, one which it is necessary to redefine what our behaviour should be in the face of situations in which the built-up groups need adaptation and not the dissonances which are characteristic of varied architectural egos. In the face of the anonymous architecture that can be observed in the house in Quinta do Lago that serves to define structures that pose on the plane of the roof (dome, pyramid),. This revision that is being made at this time serves to solve gaps , corners, flights, plane changes. Hopefully Souto can find more situations, such as A Caida, so that he may be able to continue analyzing in an extraordinarily interesting and timely field.

Souto recognizes that he is a tireless worker. The poet Sophia de Mello wrote that poetry asked her for a "dense and compact obstinacy". The passion along with the obstinacy or perseverance of Eduardo, together with the continuity summarizes his work. Souto de Moura talks about the suitability of discipline to culture, and the place, to find the reasons to think, write and build. All done with passion. As Herberto Helder wrote in "A Paixão Grega" (The Greek Passion):

Li algures que os gregos antigos não escreviam necrológios,
quando alguém morria perguntavam apenas:
tinha paixão?
quando alguém morre também eu quero saber da qualidade
da sua paixão:
se tinha paixão pelas coisas gerais,
água,
música,
pelo talento de algumas palavras para se moverem no caos,
pelo corpo salvo dos seus precipícios com destino à glória,
paixão pela paixão,
tinha?
e então indago de mim se eu próprio tenho paixão,
se posso morrer gregamente,
que paixão?[7]

7. Helder, Herberto, "A Paixão Grega", A Faca não Corta o Fogo, Assírio & Alvim, Lisboa, 2008. p. 612

A passion that does not distinguish between the small and the large. The selection of works of this issue of Archives has sought to bring together smaller-scale projects such as the chapel in Venice and others of a larger scale such as the dam. The ability that has been shown in large-scale interventions such as the Porto metro are magnificent examples of total control of the project and how sticking to very simple rules is decisive, for example the repetition in the dimension of the stone used can lead to the final result being unified and coherent, at the same time as being more cost effective. But, on the other hand, it is convenient to look with the greatest interest at his smaller projects: the first in the ruin of Gêres and the last in the chapel in Venice. Both projects are exceptional, the ruin marks the beginning of a good stage in his early years, and the chapel is not only configured as an exceptional project of Souto, it also shows some possibilities of sincere expression that venture into magnificent future projects.

24 images collected

by Souto de Moura

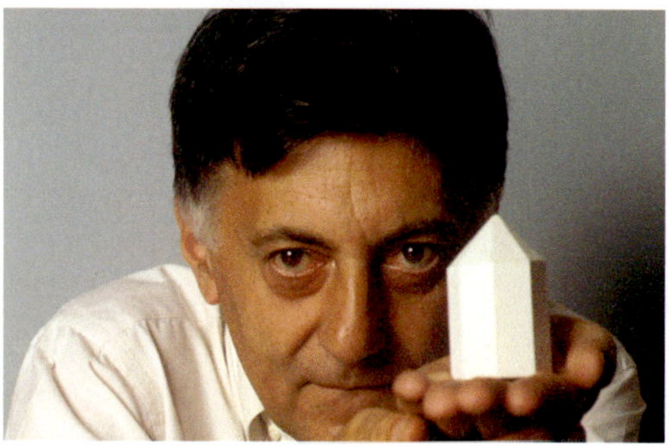

1. Paul Cézanne
2. Paul Klee
3. Mies van der Rohe
4. Enrique Vila-Matas
5. Gordon Matta Clark
6. Ahmad Jamal
7. Pedro Cabrita Reis
8. Arthur Rimbaud
9. Alvaro Siza Vieira
10. Donald Judd
11. Aldo Rossi
12. Peter Behrens
13. Johann Bernhard Fischer von Erlach
14. Álvaro Lapa
15. Fernando Pessoa
16. Claude Nicolas Ledoux
17. Karl Friedrich Schinkel
18. Angelo de Sousa
19. Glenn Gould
20. Herberto Helder
21. Jacques Herzog
22. Gian Lorenzo Bernini
23. Thomas Bernhard
24. Miles Davis

Vatican Chapel

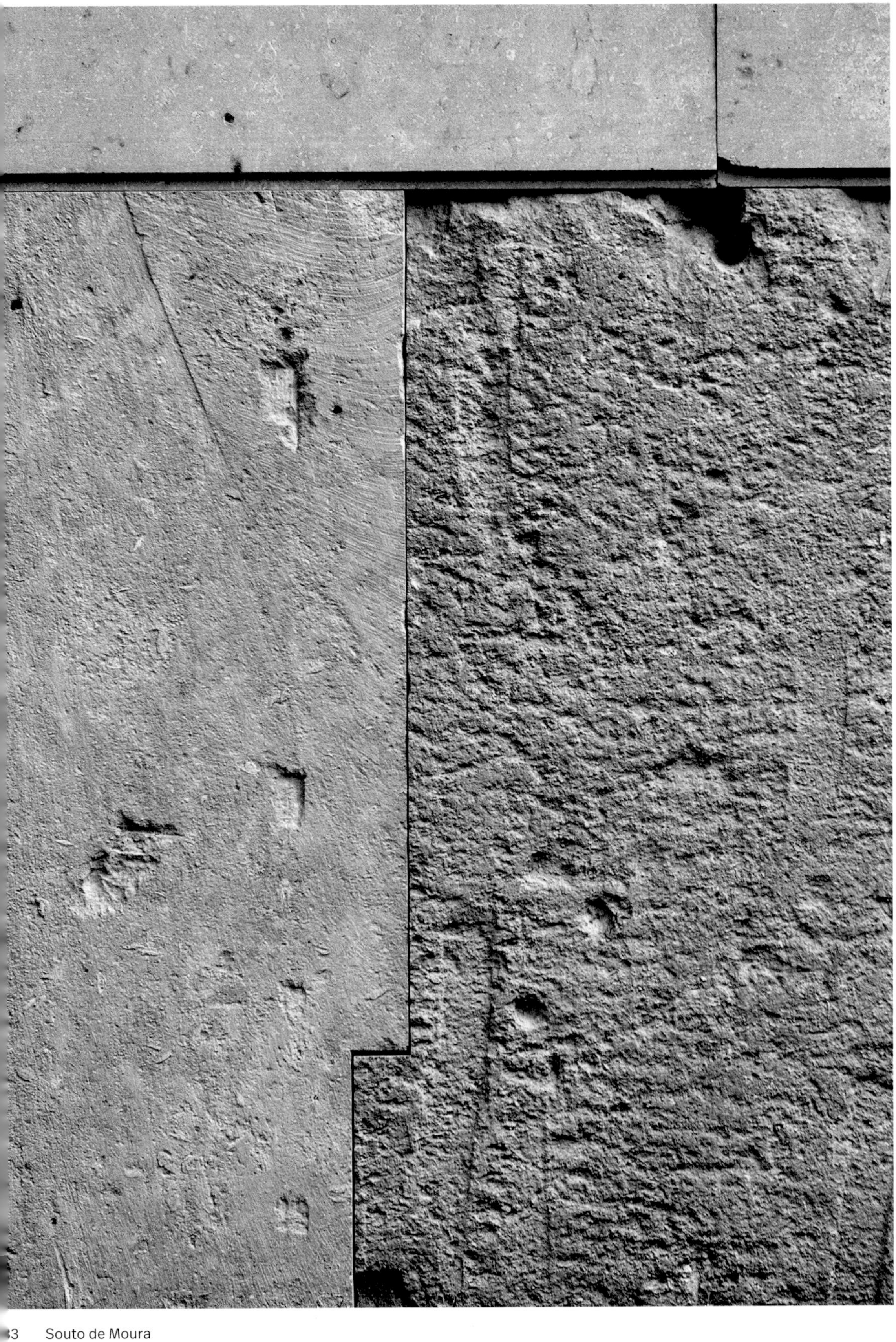

Chapel for participation of the Vatican in the Venice Biennale. San Giorgio Maggiore island, Venice, Italy
2018

No, it's not a chapel, it's not a sanctuary, and neither is it a burial mound. It's a space enclosed by stone walls, with an alter situated far from the entrance, in the widest zone. A roof partially covers the site, which has been placed upon stones which have been rammed into the ground. The entrance has been placed with reference to an existing tree. The inside of the walls have a second stone that functions as seats or supports no matter what the ceremony. A bench to "sit and wait... wait with your feet on the earth and your head in your hands" (David Mourão Ferreira).

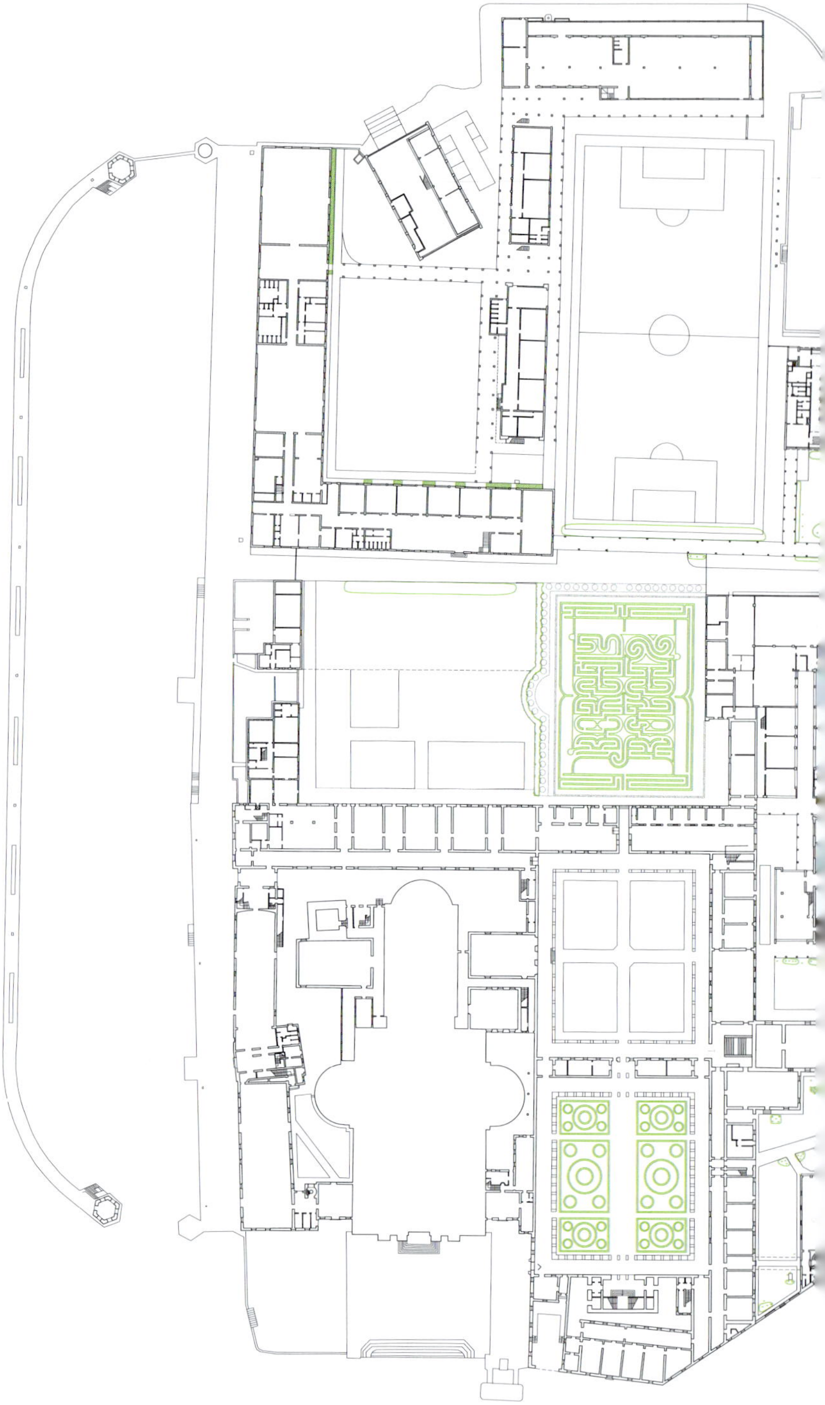

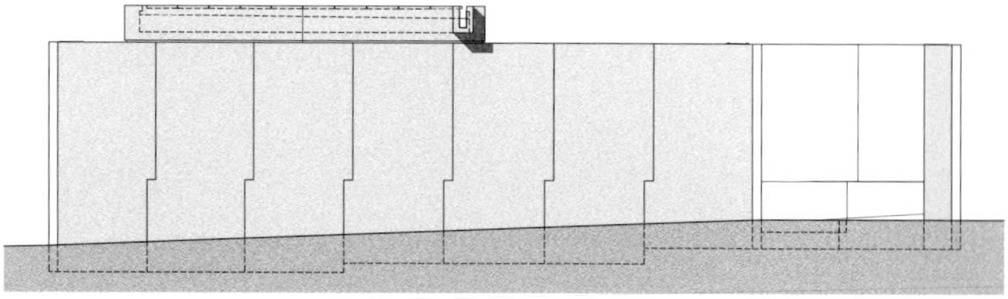

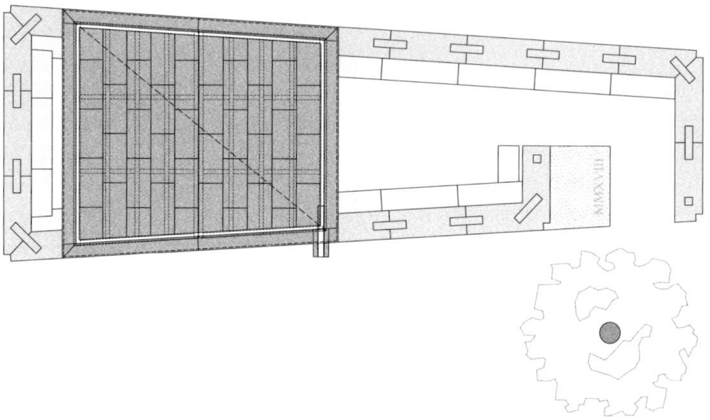

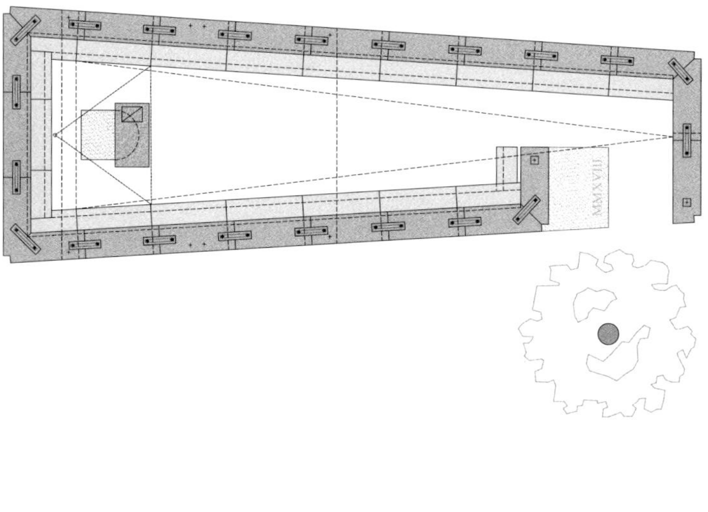

North west elevation
Roof plan
Ground plan

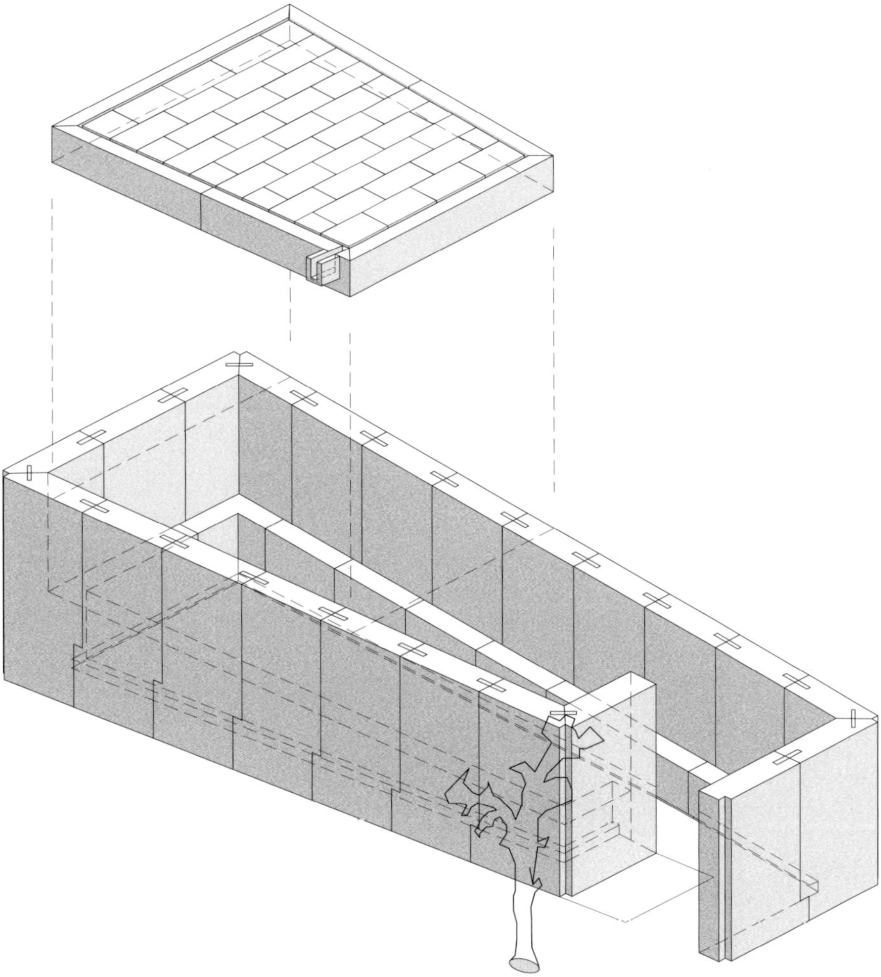

Bernardas Convent reconversion

ernardas Convent
econversion to
ousing. Tavira,
ortugal
006–2012

The Bernardas Convent was founded by the Cister in 1509 in the city of Tavira. Damaged by the Lisbon earthquake, it underwent several reforms until in 1834 it became a factory, only to later be abandoned and become a ruin. Usually the use of these ruins is associated with hotel programs, museums, or cultural centres; but so many available objects are not economically viable.

It has been decided that the convent is to be converted into a residential complex, with a functional adaptation of the existing building, rehabilitating what was still possible to maintain, and attempting to correct past errors. Homes of different sizes that are integrated into the existing structure and a new body, oriented east that takes advantage of the difference between the upper platform and the level where the old garden was located.

In the body of the church, which had already been divided into three sections, the central nave is again used as a reception area and a cafeteria has been proposed for the sacristy and other rooms. The existing structure of the tower is used to accommodate four houses of different sizes that adapt to the irregular geometry of the walls.

Within the rest of the existing walls of the convent the houses are distributed in independent modules of three different heights. The Bernardas Convent is the result of successive interventions in the original construction, extending and lengthening the original building. All the existing walls offered the use of existing holes, the reopening of windows that were closed and the opening of new windows and doors, multiplying the gaps.

The new building is half-buried, in the form of an “L”, in the eastern section; formed by a line of single-family houses of one or two floors with terraces in what used to be the orchard of the convent. The houses of this new structure look towards the salt lakes that surround them, just as the other houses do towards the salt water pool located in the great central patio.

The whole ensemble is painted to unify walls of different types, and to hide holes and the traces that these have generated. The vegetation takes centre stage, conserving the palm trees, adding trees in the central patio and climbing plants on the walls. Some metallic pergolas with vegetation provide the houses with shade and help to hide cars and facilities.

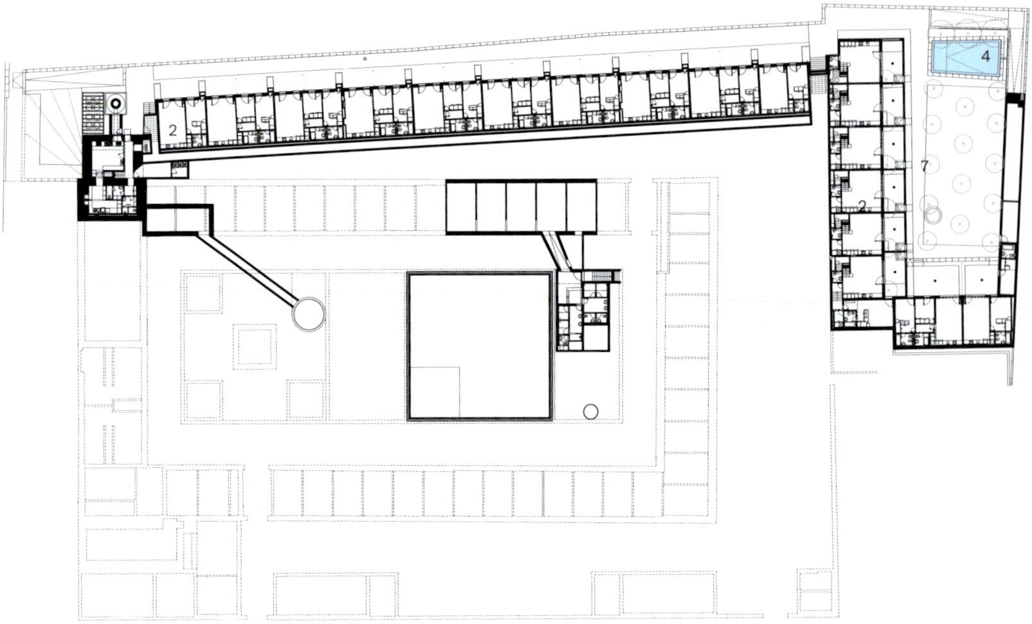

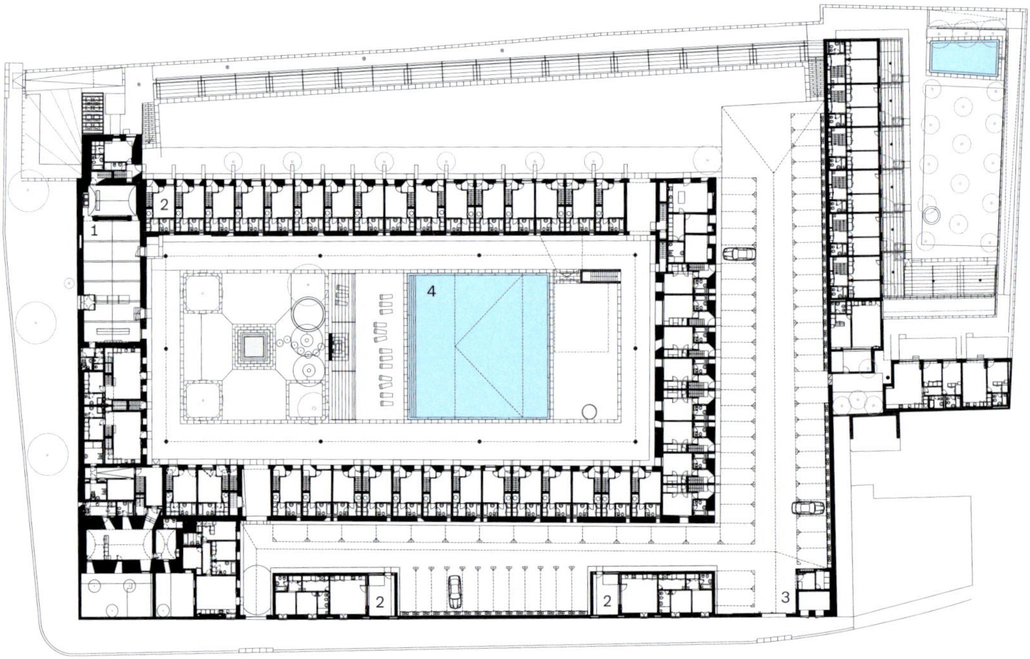

Level -1
Level 0

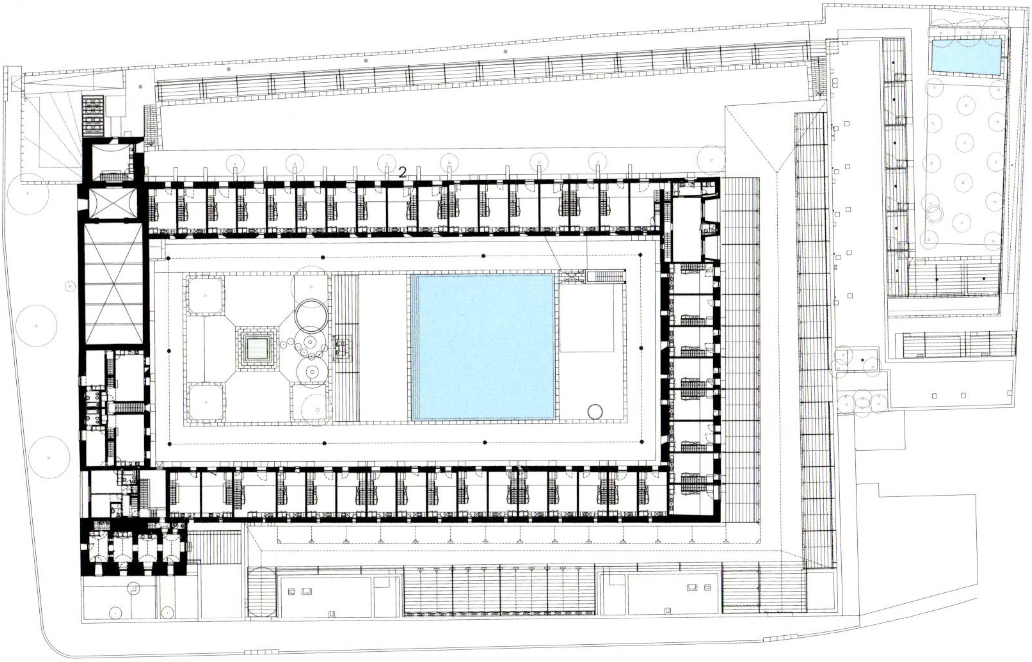

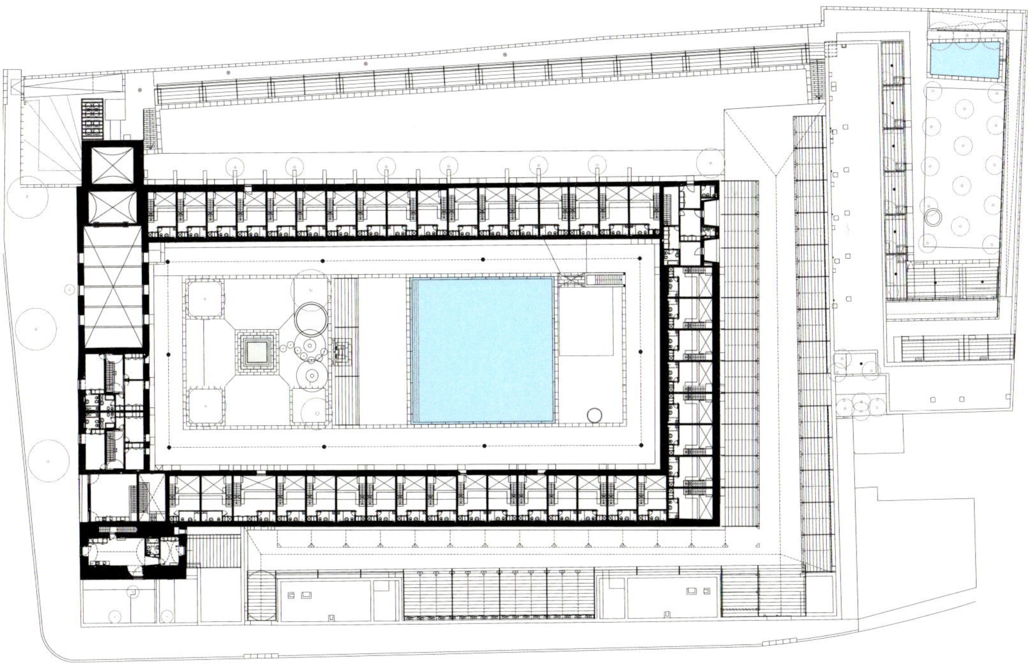

1. Restaurant (former church)
2. Apartments
3. Entrance/Technical area
4. Pool

Level 1
Level 2

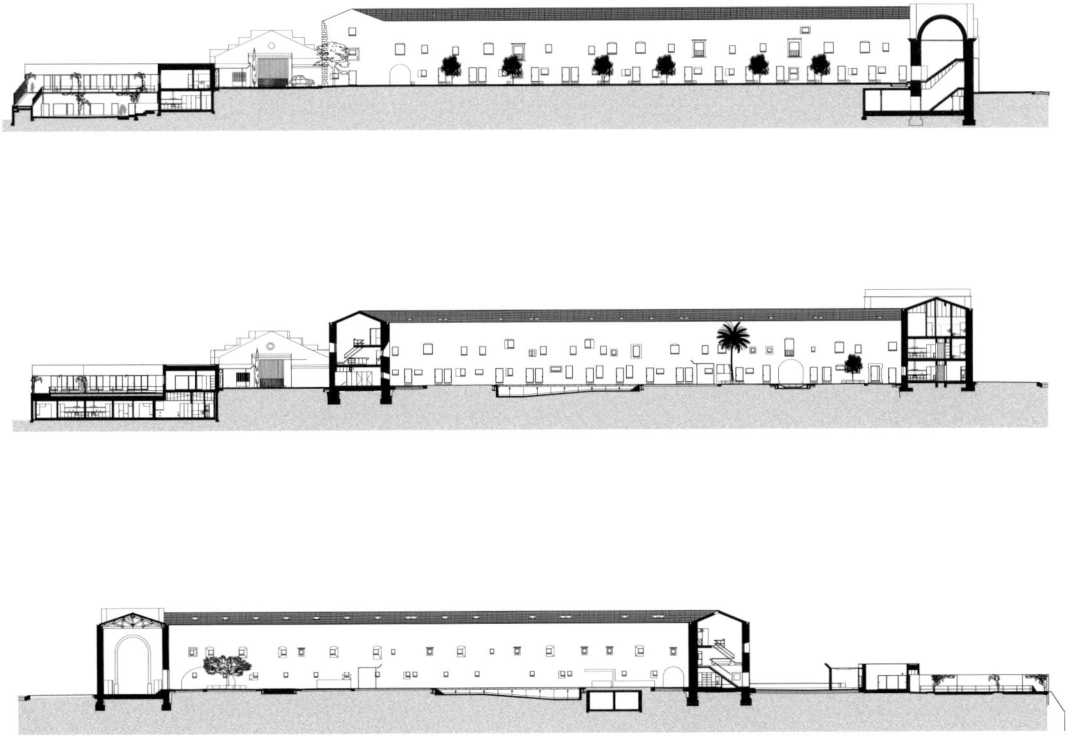

Longitudinal sections

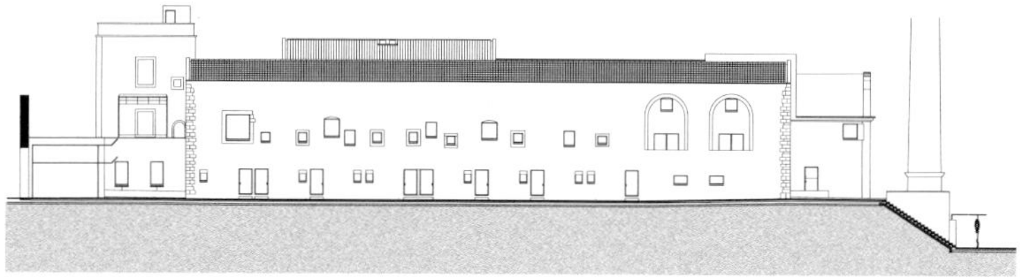

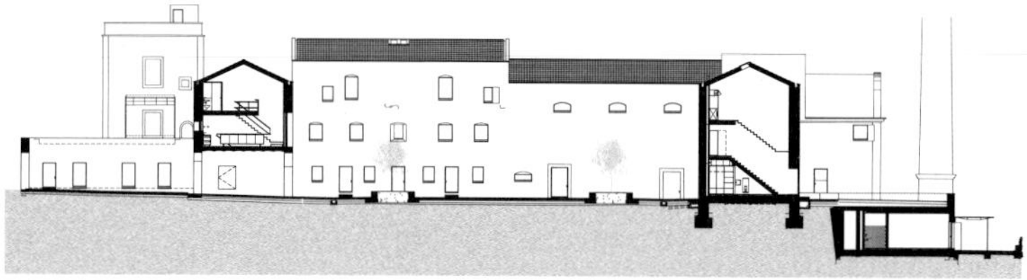

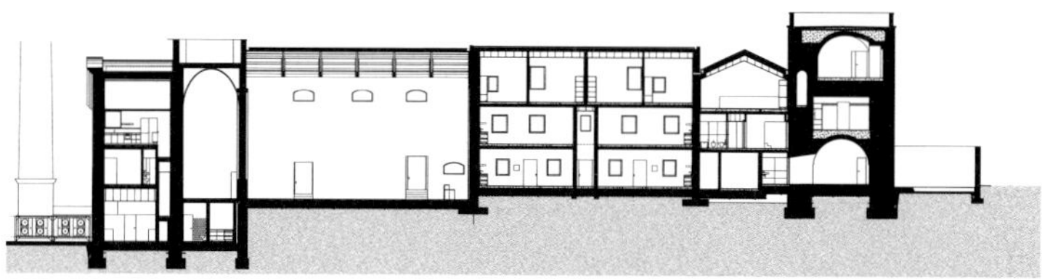

Souto de Moura Bernardas Convent reconversion

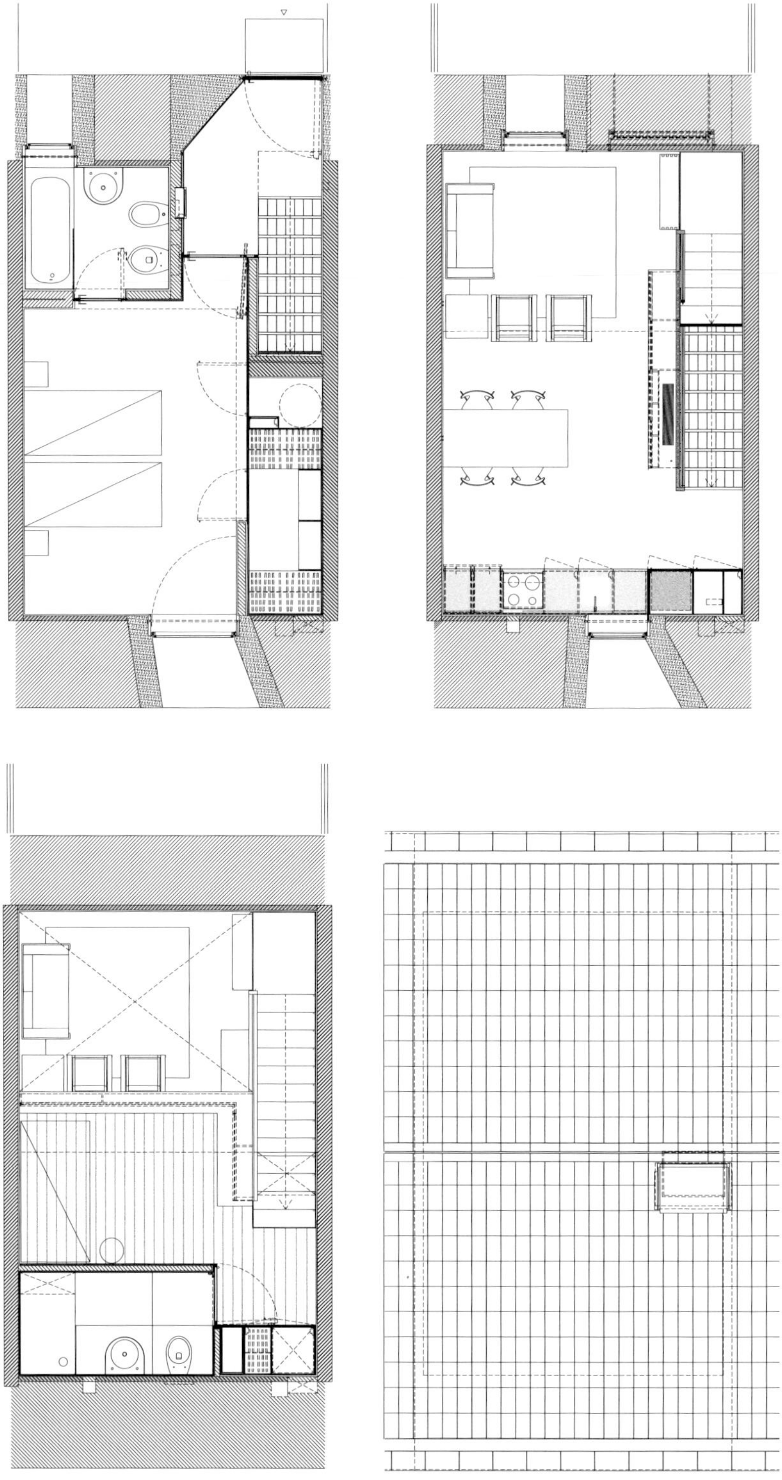

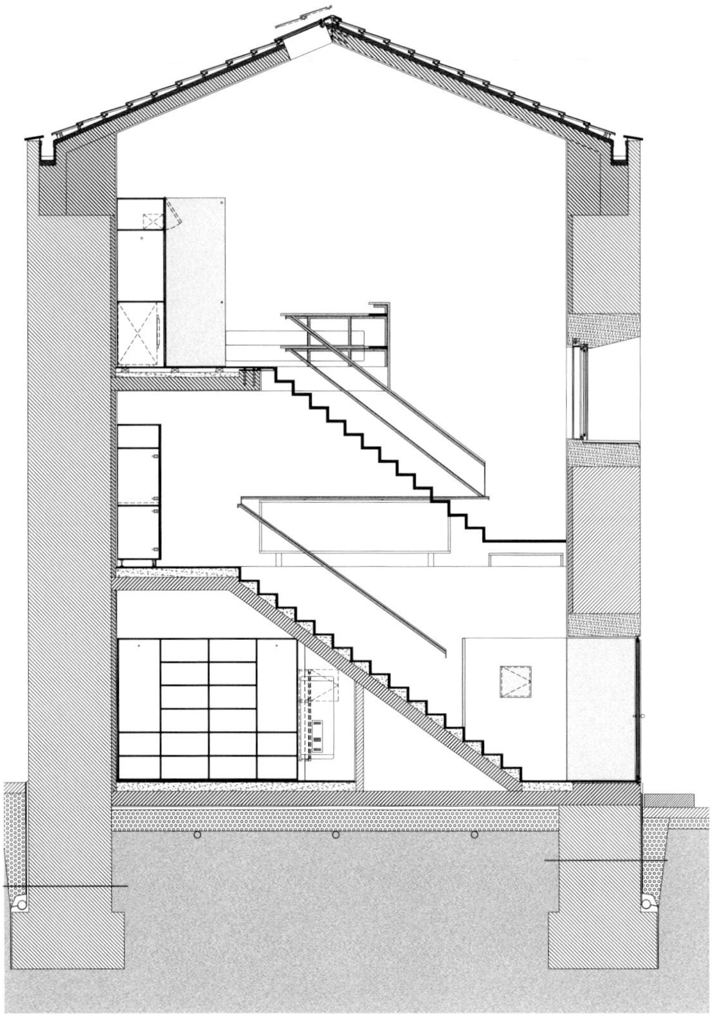

South wing typology secti

São Lourenço do Barrocal

econversion of the
gricultural buildings
f the São Lourenço
o Barrocal Resort
ɔ a tourist complex.
eguengos de
lonsaraz, Portugal
008–2016

São Lourenço do Barrocal is a country estate that grew in the nineteenth century and thus became a small village that has its own hierarchy: a street, a square, outbuildings, cloisters. A combination that is rare to see in such good condition. Located in a landscape of the Alentejo, formed by oaks, vineyards and olive groves, the centre is characterized by seven buildings arranged along a central street, which defines two main groups (North and South). The North complex consists of two buildings: the old industrial and office building and the warehouse of agricultural tools. The South complex had 5 buildings: the main house, the agricultural pavilions, the aviary, the kennel and the pigsty. Further south, the orchard area and the outdoor pool that retains a granite outcrop *(barrocal)*.

The project of transforming this complex into a place for tourists tries to find a balance between the existing situation and the adjustment to the new one. Each of the buildings has been adapted to the new program with minor modifications, with an awareness that the only way to preserve the heritage is to use it.

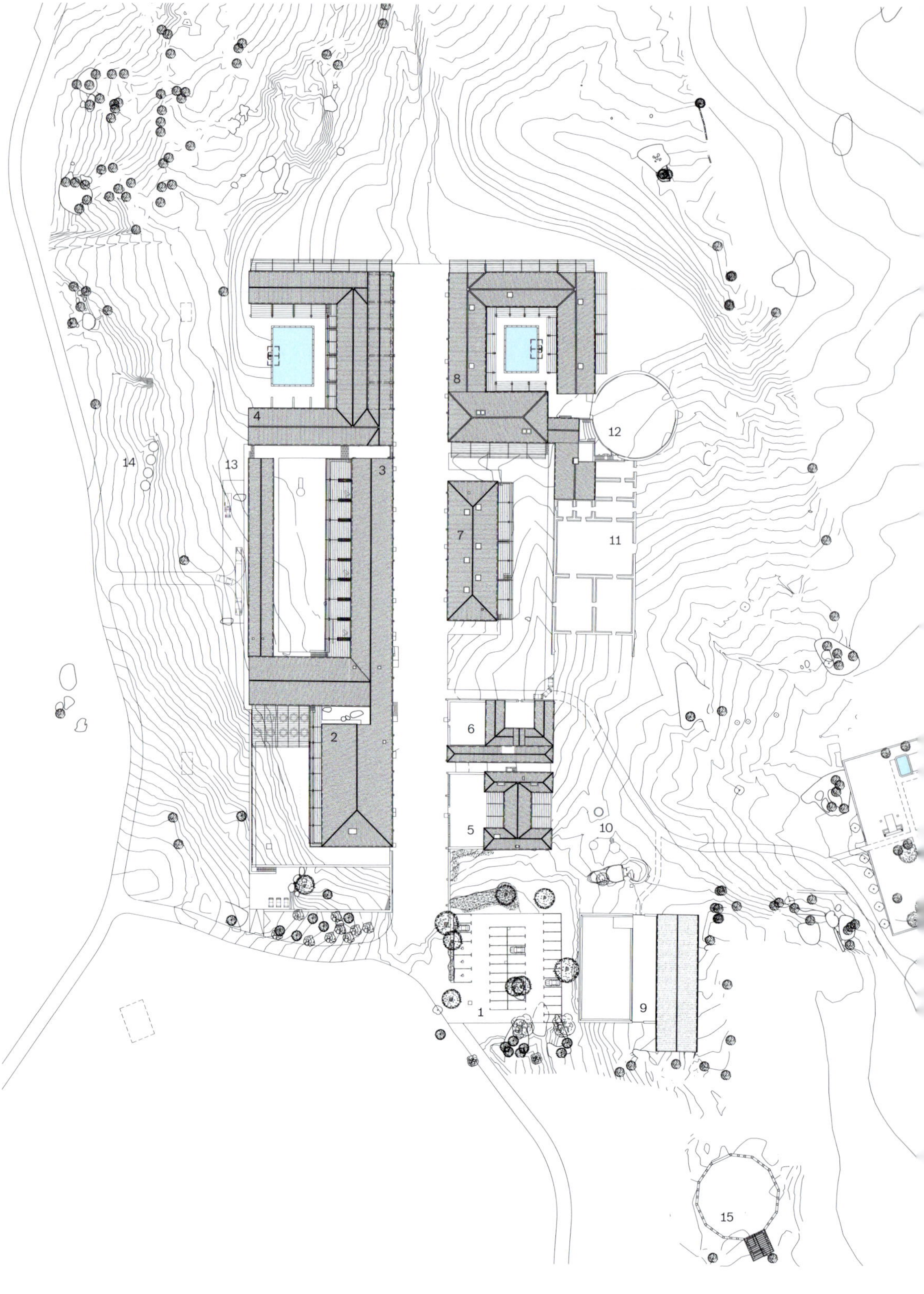
14
13
4
3
2
8
12
7
11
6
5
10
1
9
15

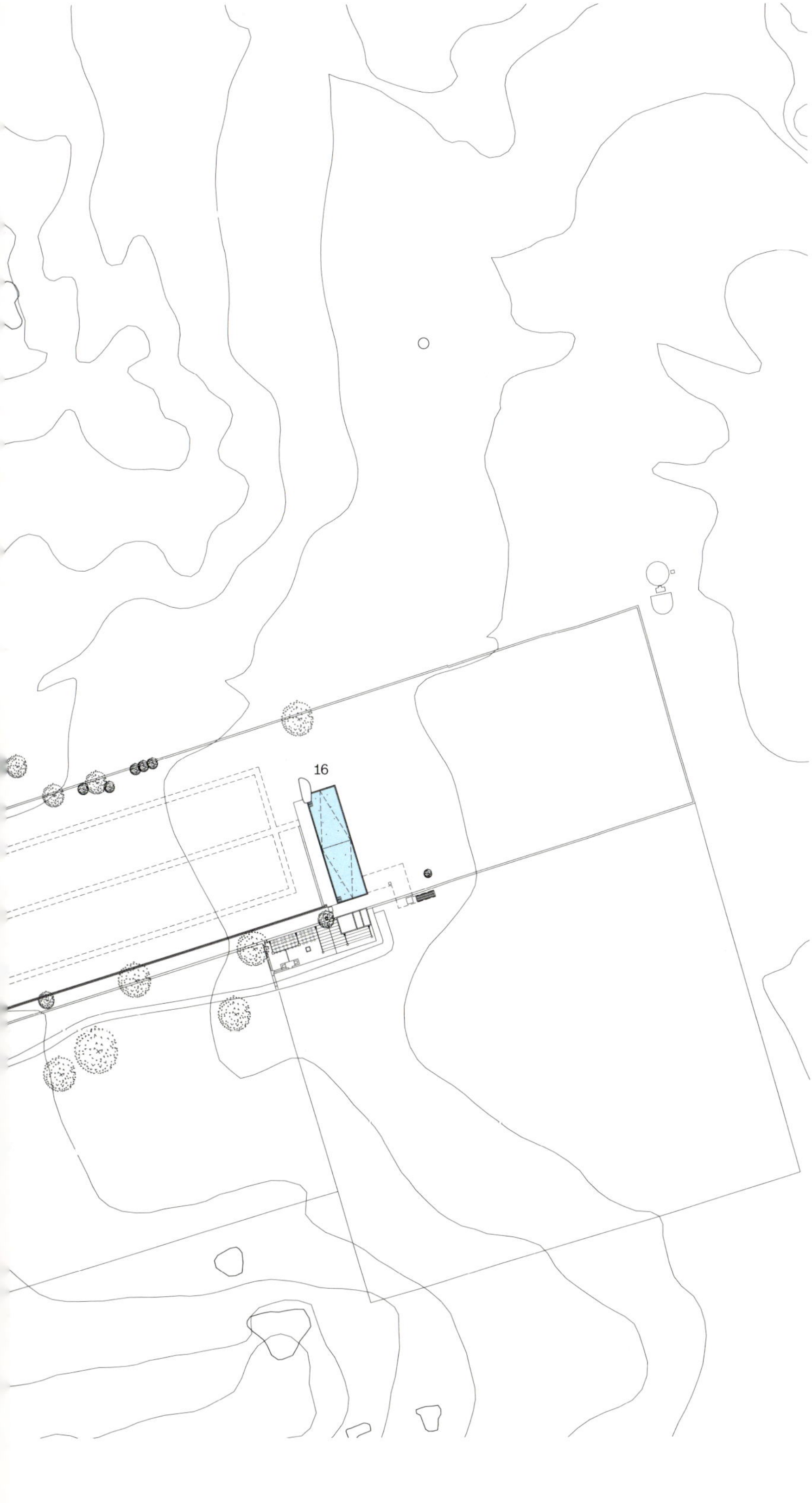

1. Parking
2. Reception/Bar (former winery)
3. Hotel/Rooms (former housekeepers' house)
4. Hotel/Rooms (former agricultural tools storage area)
5. Restaurant (former kennel)
6. Shop and children area (former dovecote)
7. Hotel/Houses (former main house)
8. Hotel/Houses (former barn)
9. Stable (former barn)
10. Water tanks
11. Garden (former cattle park)
12. Garden (former bull ring)
13. Cellar (former storage)
14. Grain silos
15. Garden (former bee yard)
16. Pool

Souto de Moura São Lourenço do Barrocal

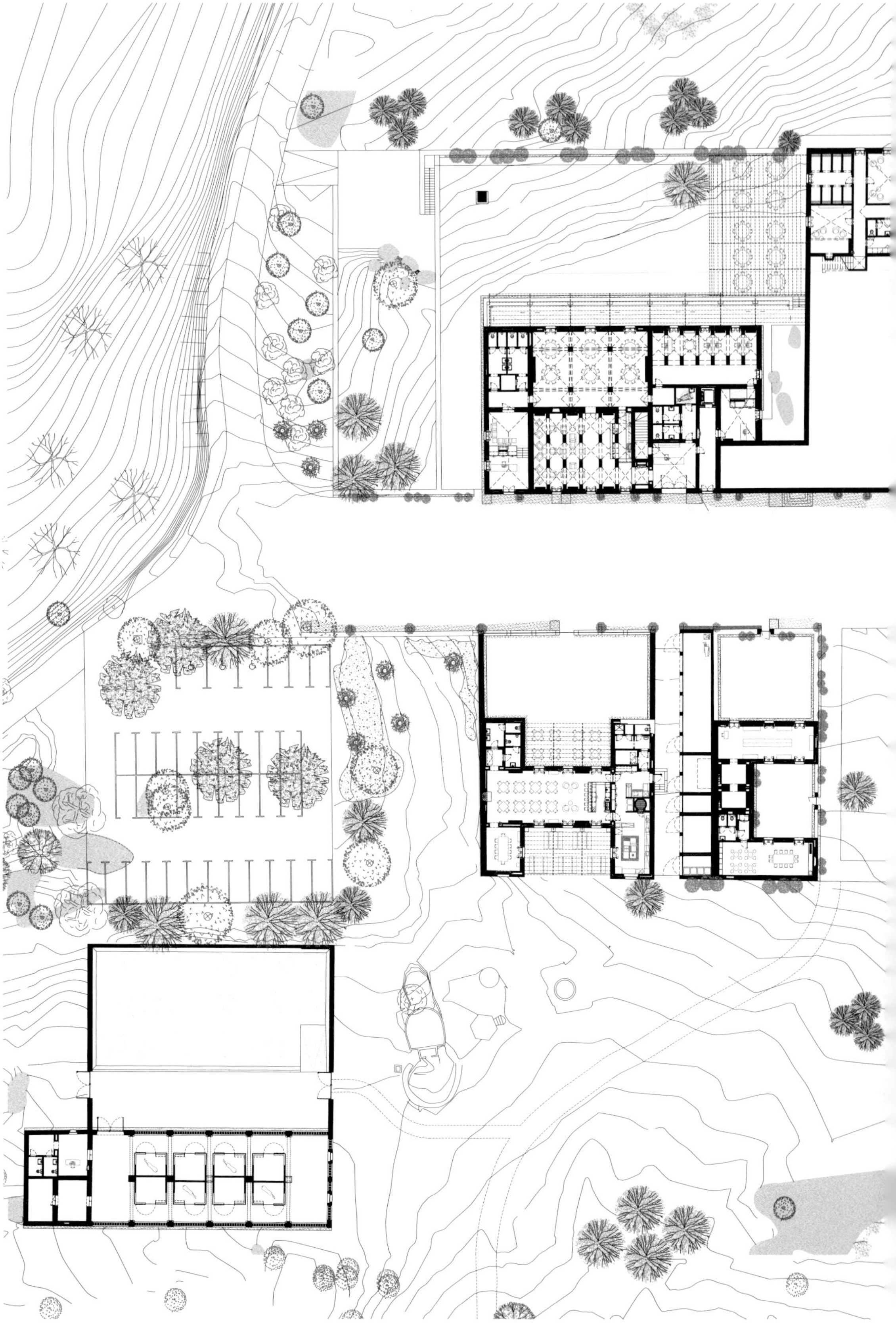

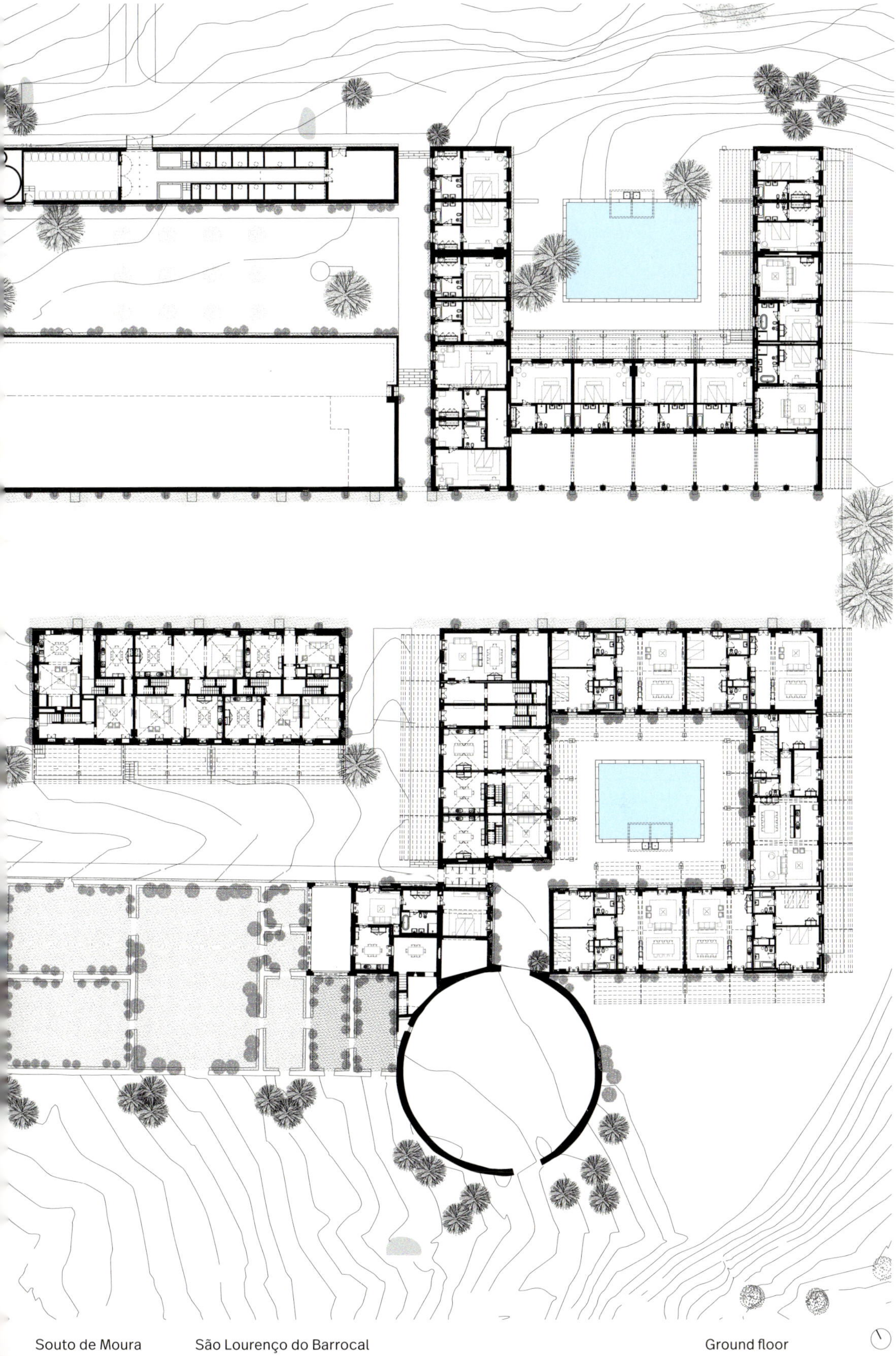

Souto de Moura São Lourenço do Barrocal Ground floor

Souto de Moura São Lourenço do Barrocal

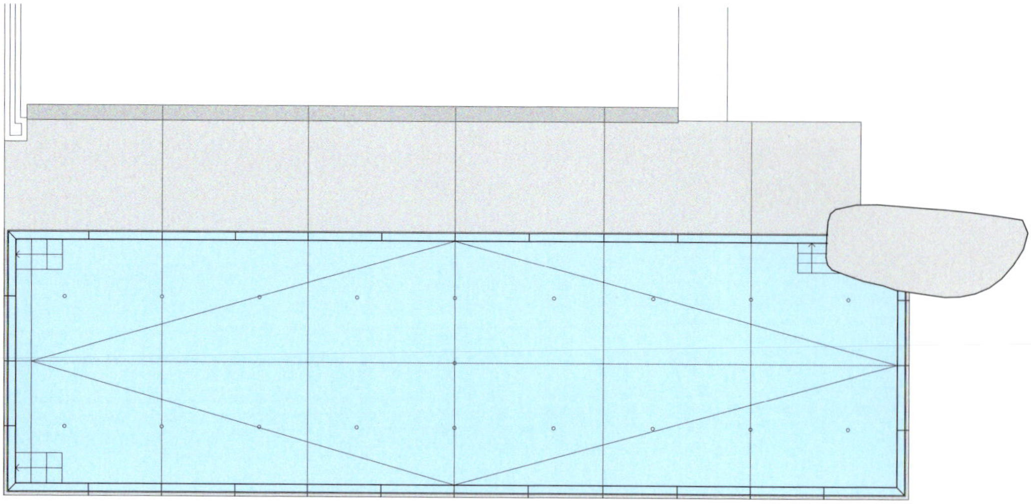

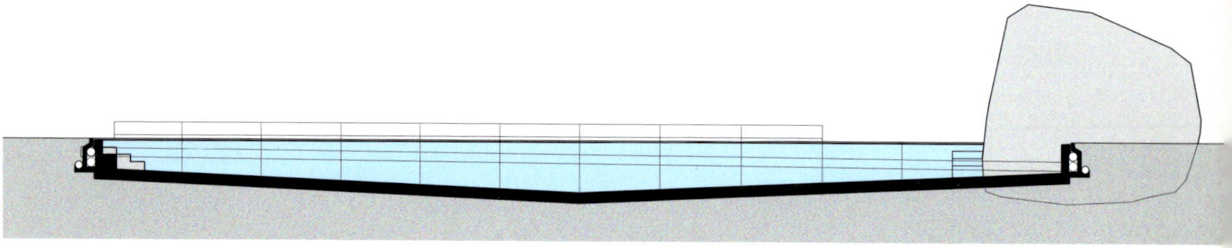

Swimming pool detail

Souto de Moura São Lourenço do Barrocal

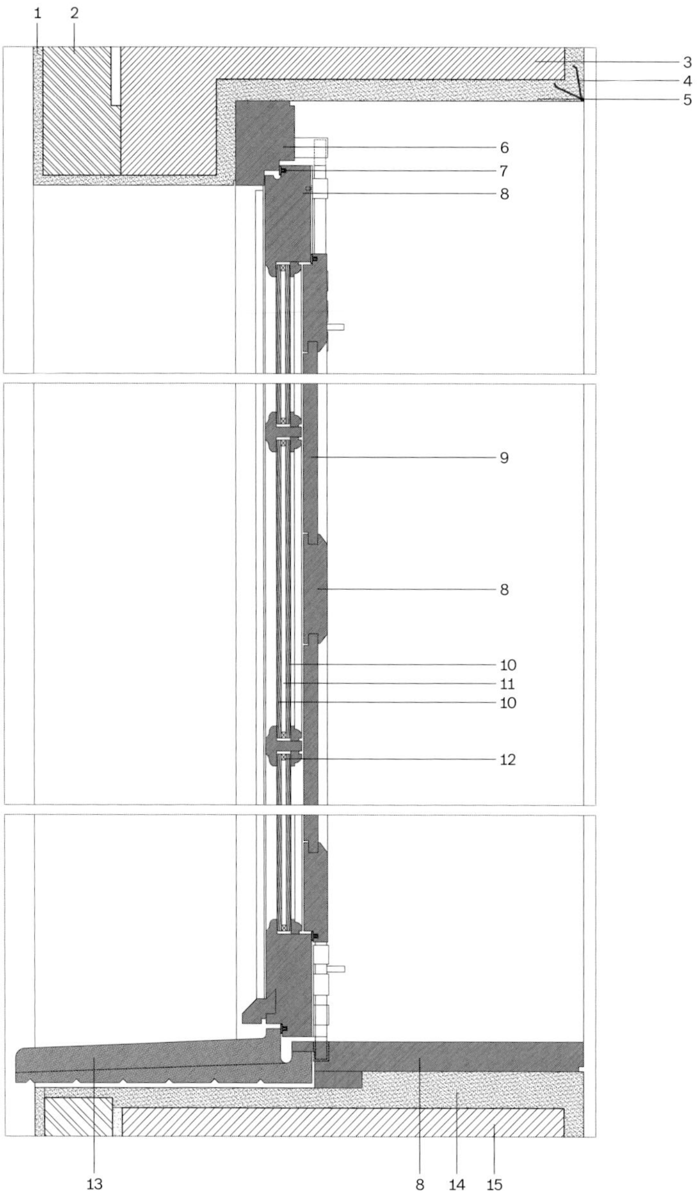

1. Traditional brick wall equal to pre-existent
2. DDL type screed
3. Reinforced concrete lintel
4. DDL type plaster
5. PVC Corner profile
6. Solid wood frame
7. Rubber stopper
8. Solid wood
9. Solid wood cushion
10. Glass 4 mm
11. Air space 5 mm
12. Low-profile seal painted grey
13. Solid wood sill
14. Screed
15. Brick wall

Window detail

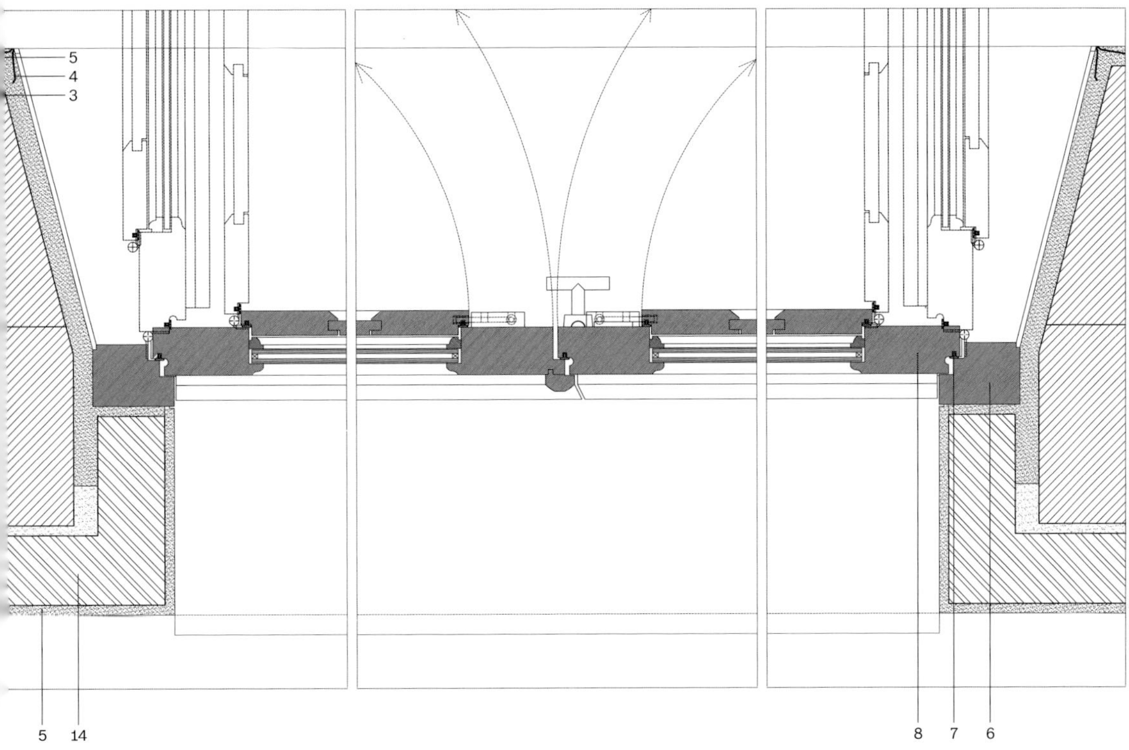
5
4
3
5
14
8
7
6

Hotel and Catering School & Robinson Foundation

Eduardo Souto de Moura with Graça Correia

econversion of the old obinson Foundation) a Hotel and Catering chool & Robinson oundation. Eduardo outo de Moura ith Graça Correia. ortalegre, Portugal 004–2009

The move of the Robinson cork factory to the new industrial zone of Portalegre generated an empty space of almost 60,000 m² in an important metropolitan development area of the city. An area constructed with hangers, warehouses and workshops, in addition to the main area that defines its front. The rehabilitation program of the old factory's facilities attempts to recuperate its historical connection with the city, redefining the functions of various buildings and recovering a notable industrial heritage. The plan introduces squares, walkways and facilities, allowing for an articulation between the buildings of the Robinson factory and the existing urban fabric, all this being physically marked by the tear corresponding to the opening of street.

An activity destined to guarantee the survival of the original implementation with the successive and necessary extensions which will be undertaken on the basis of a principal additive which would add order to all of the industrial complex. This, formed by the buildings that are already available along a type of walkway, will now configure a new relationship with the surrounding area through the strategic implantation of new buildings for the Hotel and Catering School and a first auditorium, which will contribute to the clear definition of a street which is understood in its urban form.

Within the plan, the location of the parking lot is fundamental. The structure allows for different activities to take place, not just parking.

The auditorium has the dual function of closing the line of constructions that have been adapted for the International Virtual Reality Centre and a second auditorium, and at the same time it creates a reference to the shape of the street. It is an unit which is there essentially to support the Hotel and Catering School working together with the second auditorium. One of the premises of the plan is the combined usage of the infrastructures. The auditorium was thought of with a constructive system and the image of a "metallic machine"—a sculpture which marks its presence within the industrial complex.

To the south, the Hotel and Catering School building has been thought of as a box which is supported by the terrain, defining a large balcony to which all the main spaces of the school open at the same time—classrooms, library, lounge, restaurant and bar. To the north the box is closed towards the street.

The proposal of all the complex takes on a risk in trying to correct the critical situation of messiness in the current urban growth of Portalegre, re-evaluating its resources and potential. In the implementation strategy for the new buildings, the resource of the iconographic element present in the common memory was considered to be the chimneys which is highlighted in the profile of the city.

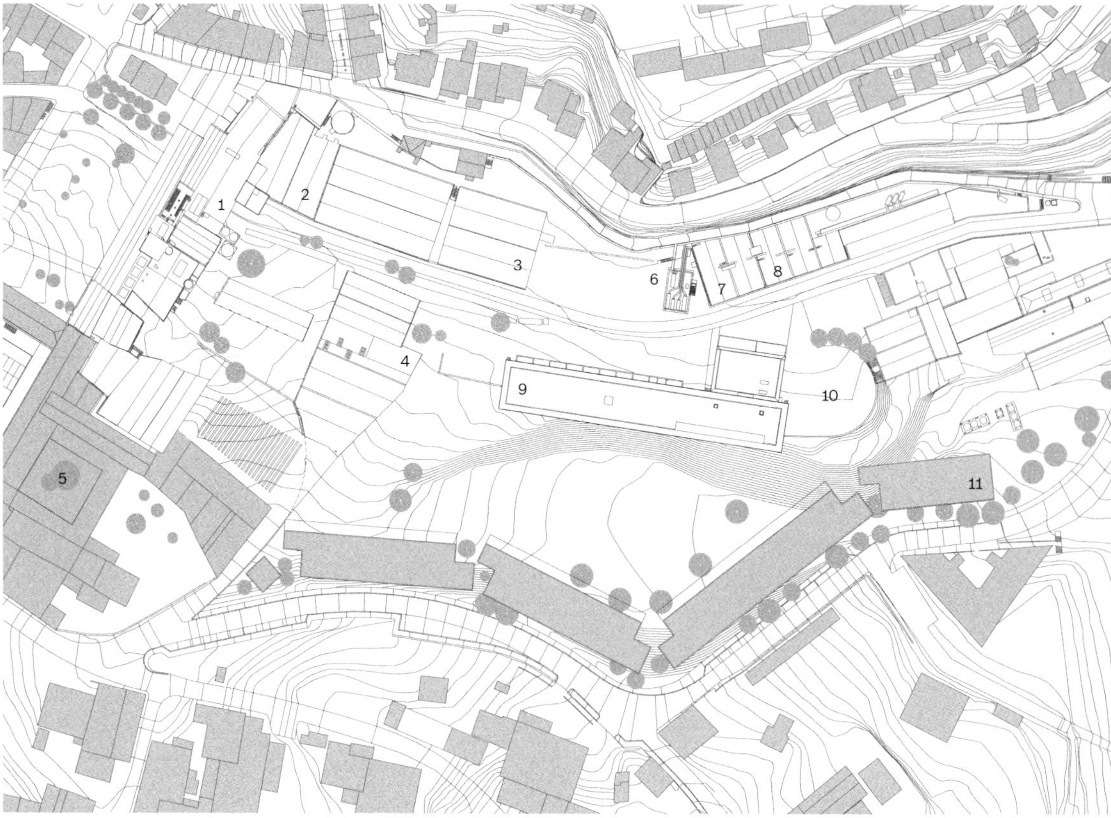

1. Cork museum
2. Firefighter museum
3. Parking
4. Art museum and artist residence
5. San Francisco Convent
6. Auditorium A
7. Auditorium B
8. Virtual reality centre
9. Hotel and Catering School
10. Students square
11. Residential area

Site plan

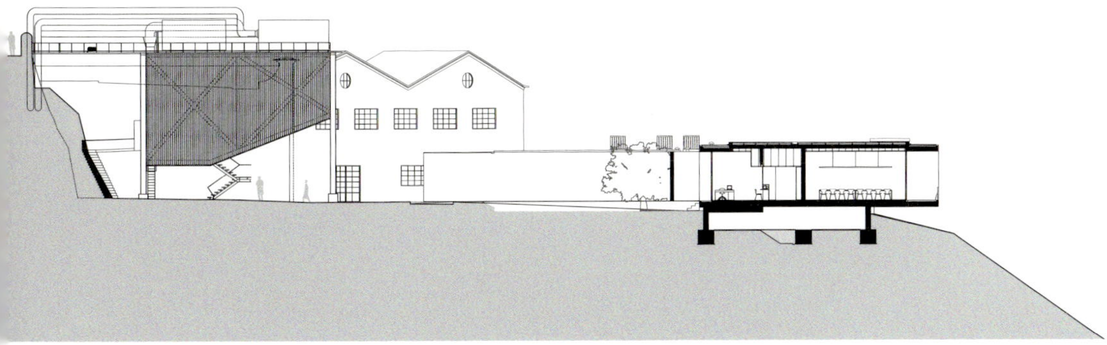

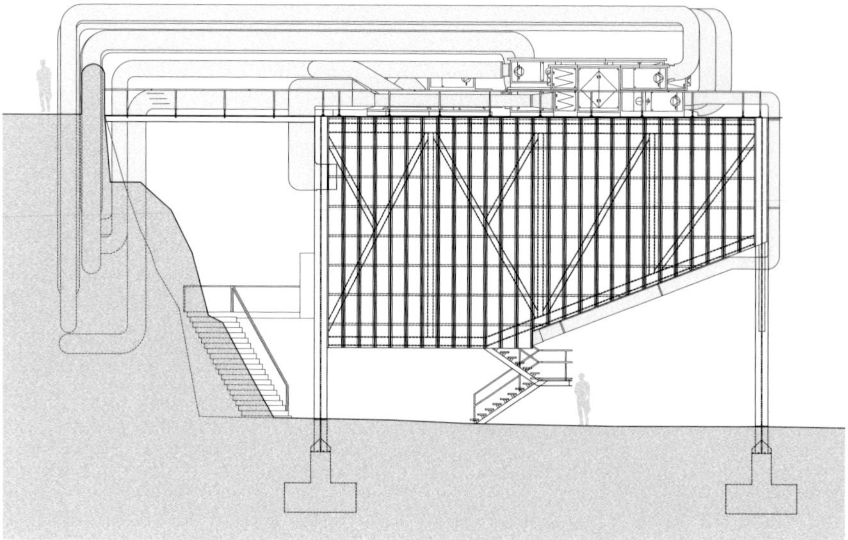

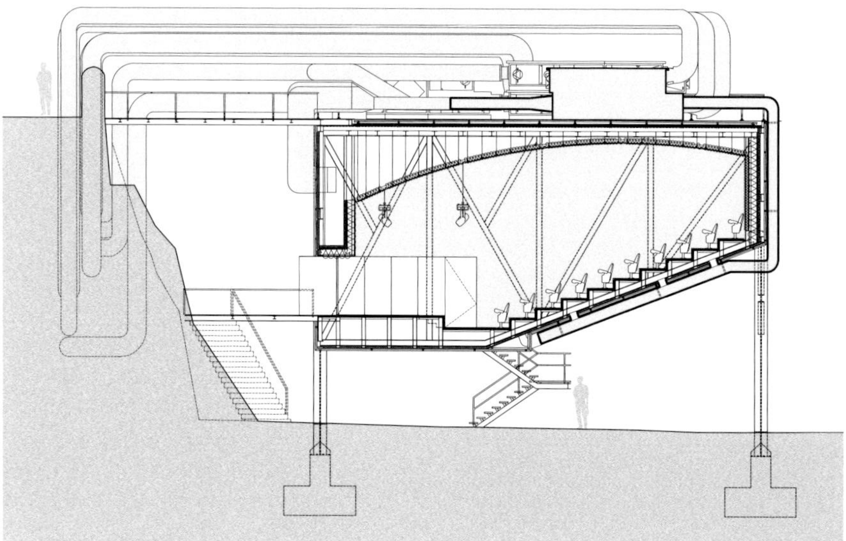

West elevation
Longitudinal section

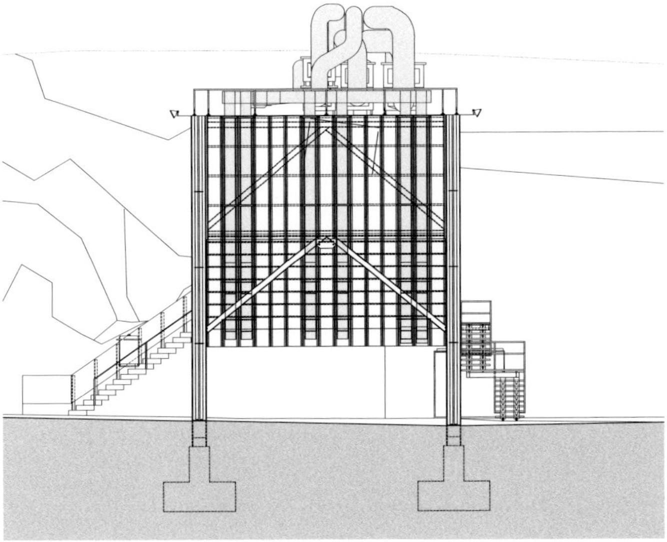

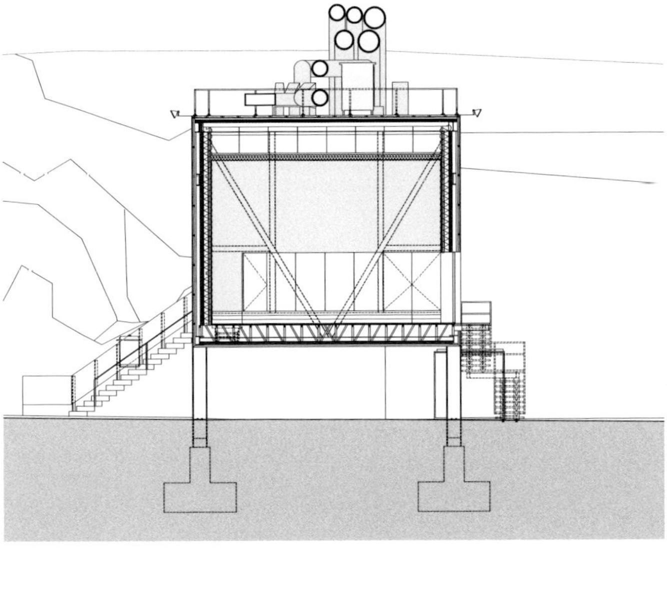

South elevation
Transversal section

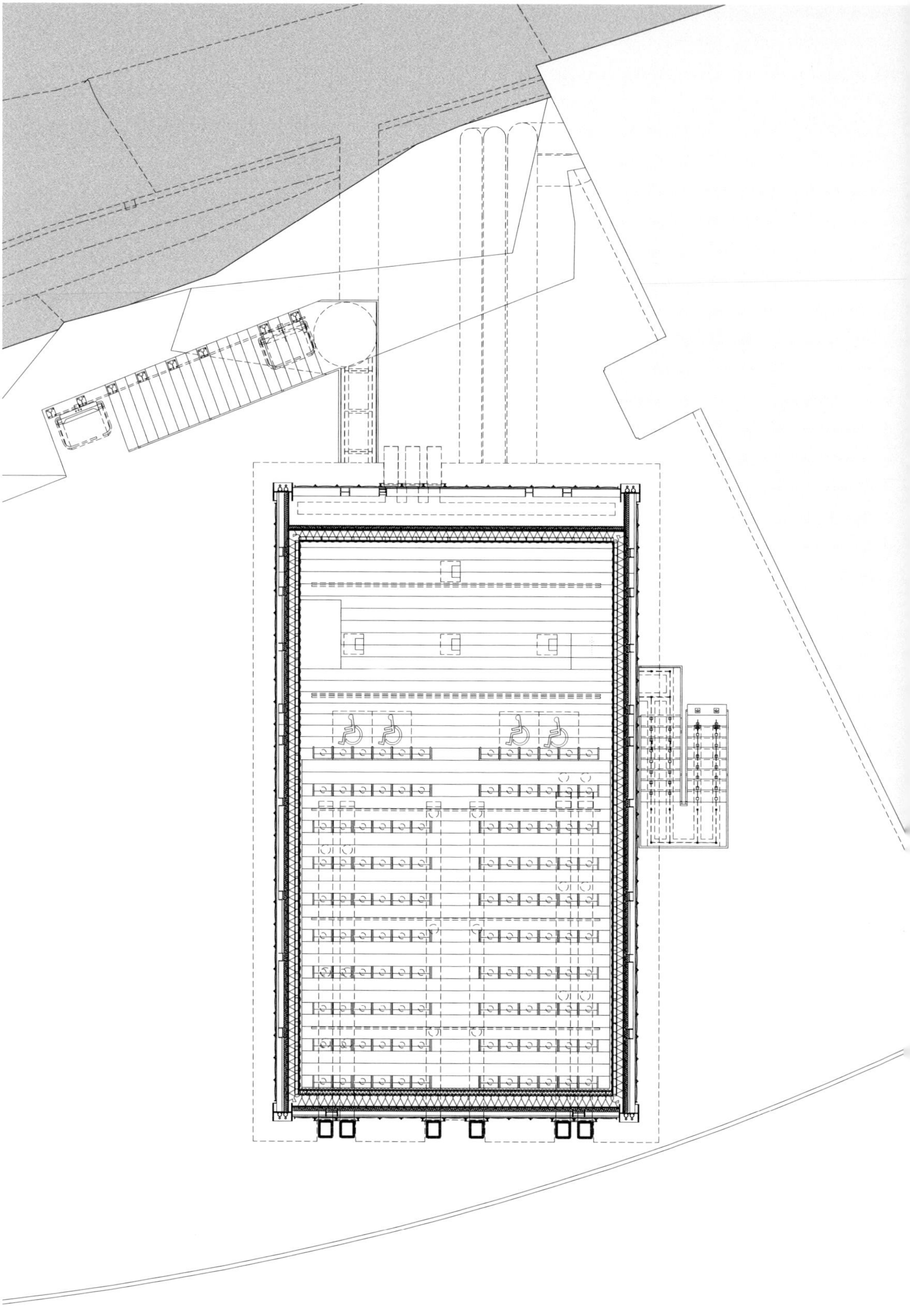

Auditorium plan

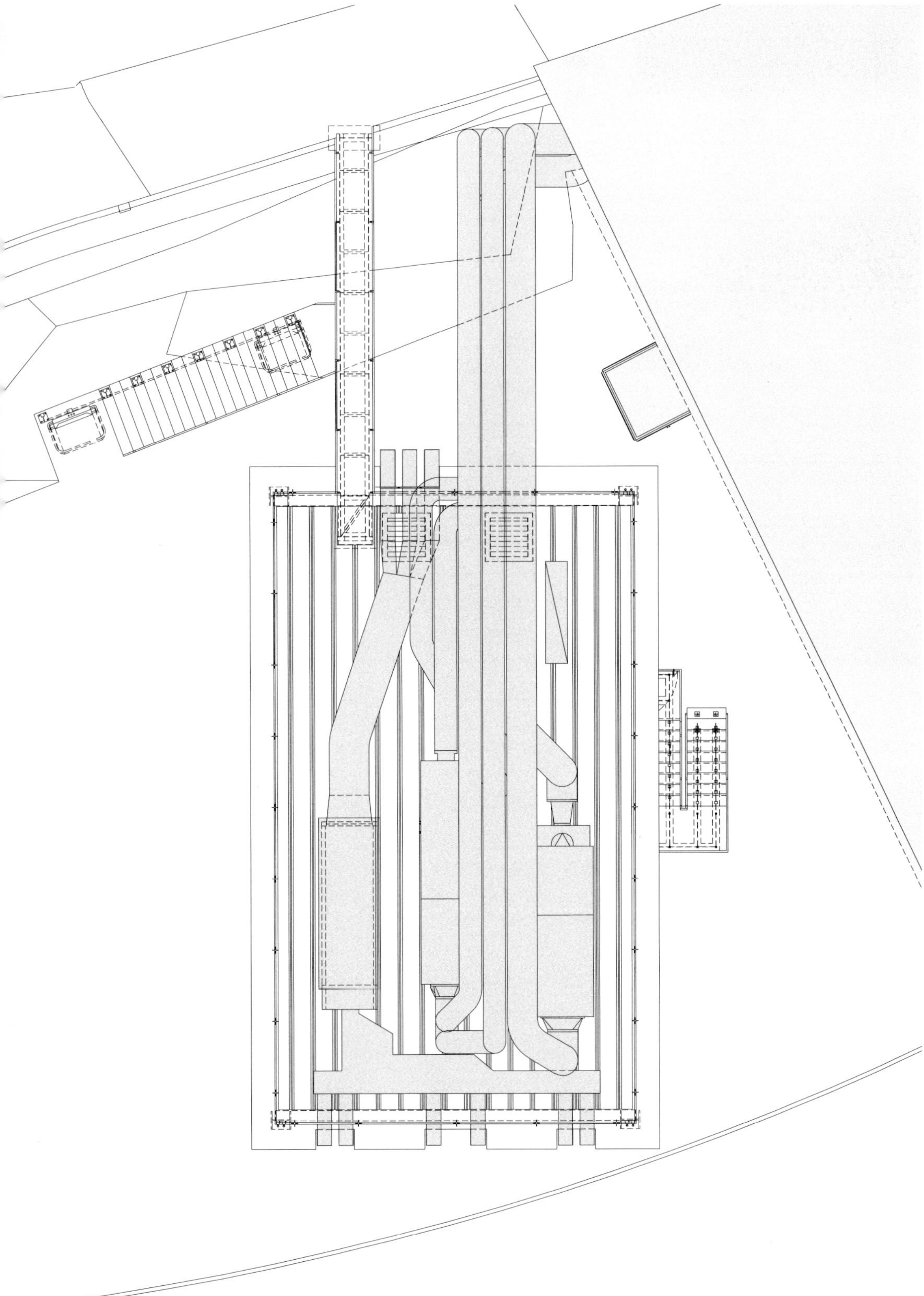

HeliMac
HeliMac

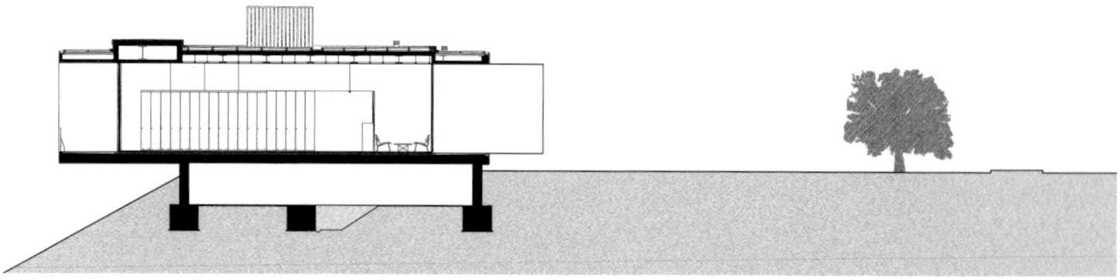

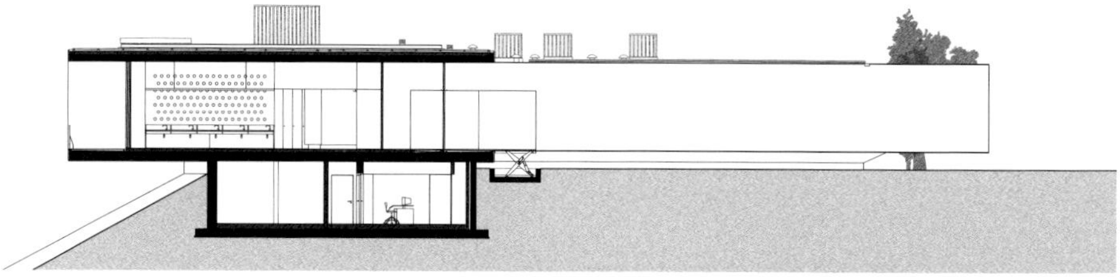

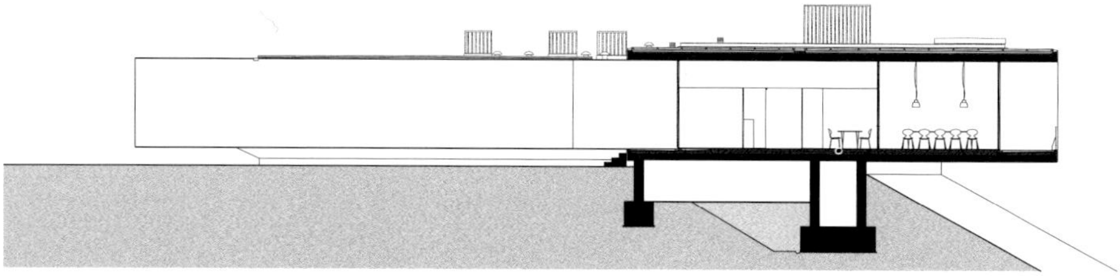

P

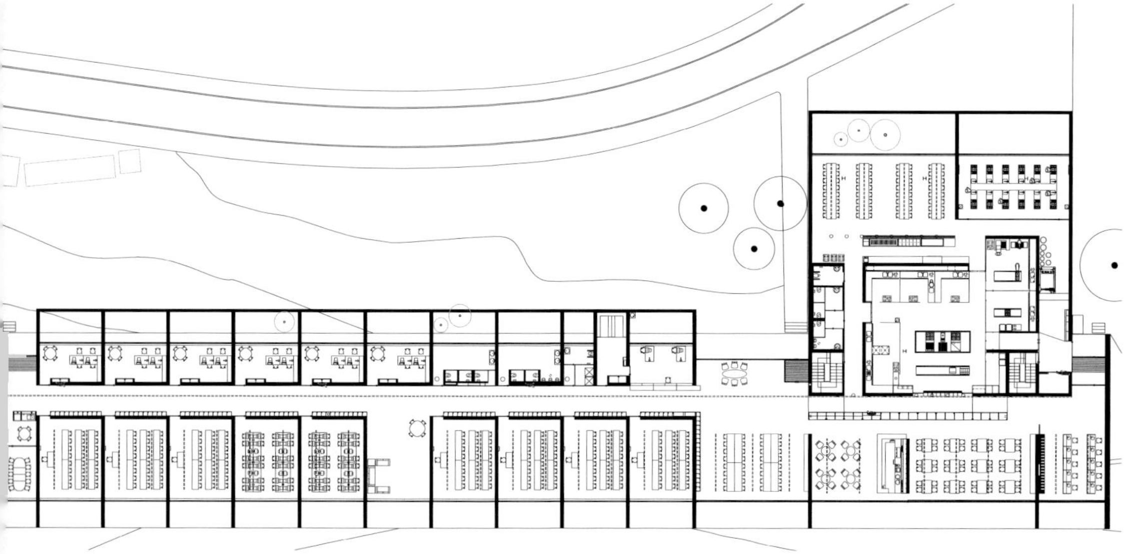

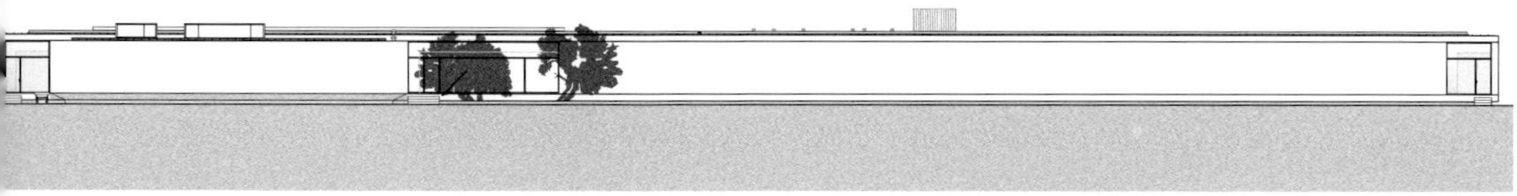

South elevation

Cultural centre Espaço Miguel Torga

ESPAÇO MIGUEL TORGA

Cultural centre Espaço Miguel Torga with an area for parking and a space for open-air activities. Sabrosa, Portugal
2007–2011

The cultural centre Espaço Miguel Torga is used to study and promote the poetic and literary works of Miguel Torga. It is based in the south of an old fairground, located close to the poet's childhood home, and encircled by two converging longitudinal roads. The building sits directly next to both roads and is located between two spaces of differing characteristics: in the north, there is a paved zone in which the fairs are held once every two weeks, and in the south, a vineyard. Northward, 35 trees have been planted in the shape of a grid, which forms the layout of the market and also the car park on the other days. The building is defined by its shale walls (a characteristic element of this zone), which establish the limits between the construction and its neighbouring spaces, totally configuring its image. The slope of the terrain has been exploited and the walls extend northwards to pinpoint the fairground. Due to the sloped terrain, the walls reduce in height until they turn into benches.

Two access roads, one for the public (to the east), and one for services (to the west), are defined by a discord between the walls. The main entrance gives access to the exhibition hall, behind said hall, the library is located, along with the administration offices and the study halls. These pieces are lit from a series of private patios that are hidden by the wall of the building's northern façade. The cafeteria has a glass façade (the only one that can be perceived from the outside) with a direct entrance to allow it to function independently.

7 Souto de Moura Cultural centre Espaço Miguel Torga

1 Souto de Moura Cultural centre Espaço Miguel Torga

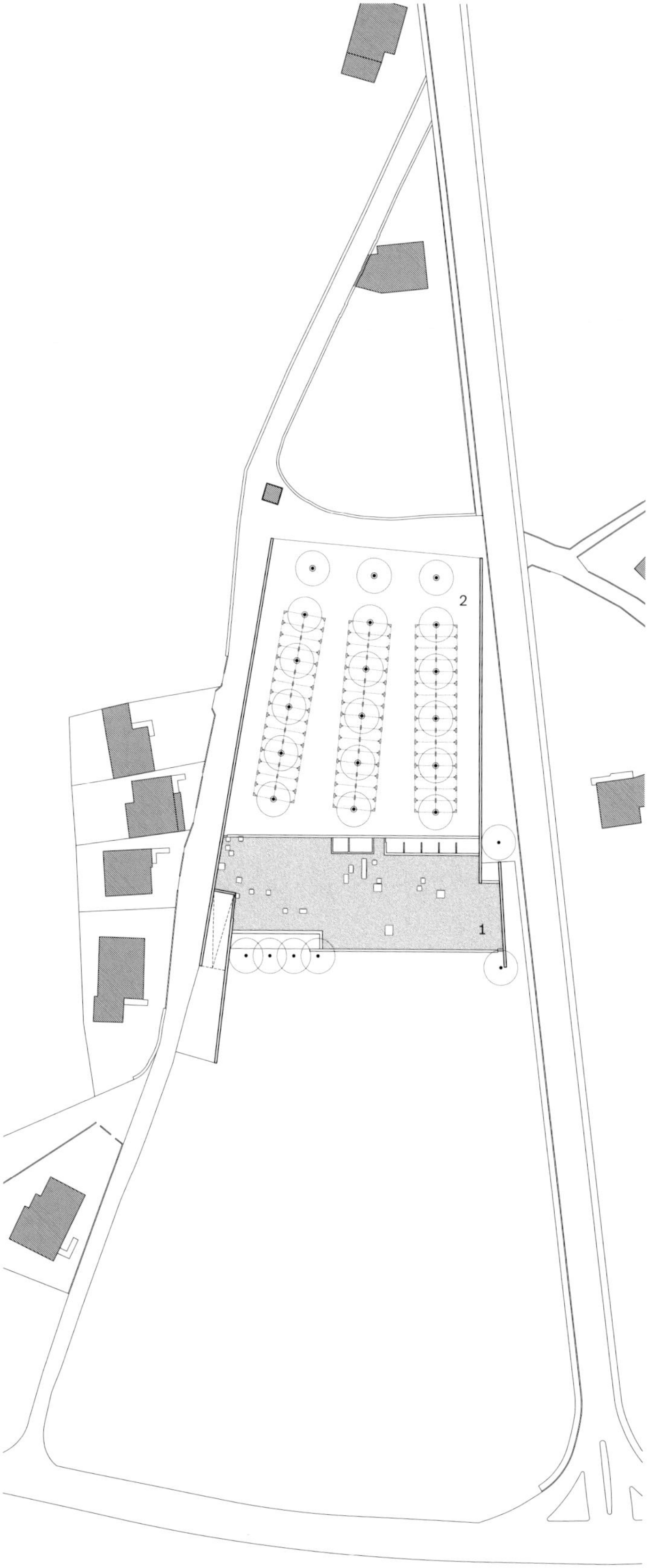

1. Cultural centre
2. Parking / Market

Site plan

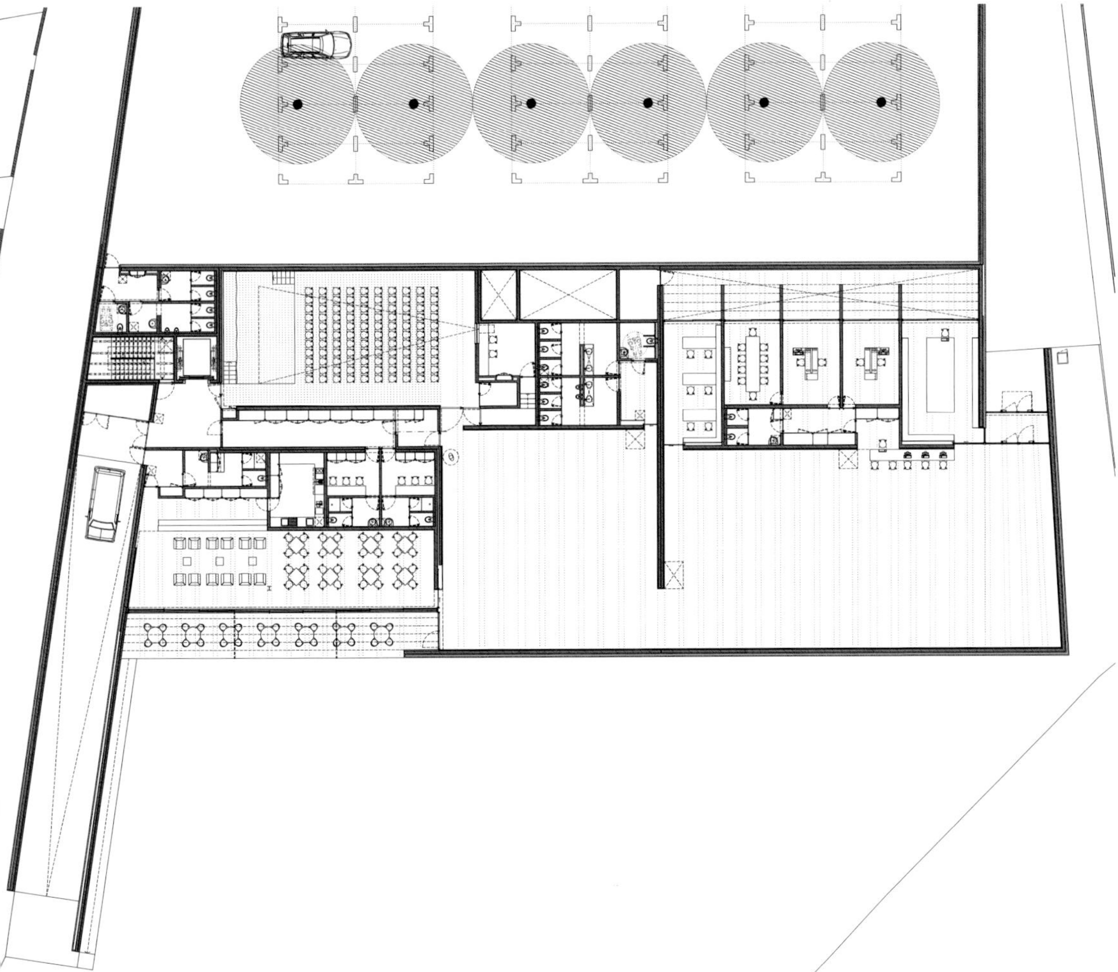

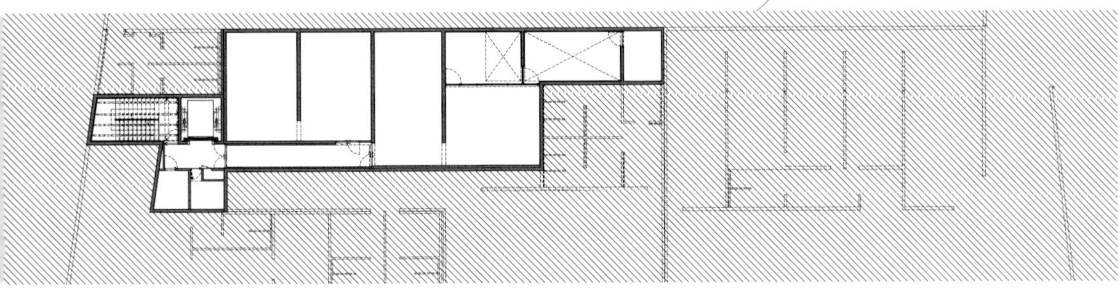

Level 0
Level -1

Multipurpose pavilion

ultipurpose pavilion
or cultural, musical,
porting and leisure
vents. Viana do
astelo, Portugal
000–2013

The multipurpose pavilion in Viana do Castelo is located on the base level of the River Lima, next to the Álvaro Siza library and aligned with the building that is designated to be the Fernando Távora leisure centre, in a prime location on the river bank. A wooded area has been placed opposite the north-west façade, tree-lined walkways mark the path towards the entrance of the pavilion and a ramp that leads to the basement. The main entrances are situated in the north-west and south-east façades. The building can honestly be defined as a table upon which an aluminium box has been placed, along with all the equipment necessary for holding the cultural, musical, sporting, and leisure activities that take place in its interior. With capacity for 4,000 people, the new building has a surface area of 3,792 metres squared separated into three floors. The court can be found in the basement along with access to the lateral grandstands. On the ground floor, an ambulatory uses glass to guarantee the transparency of the city, the river, and the interior of the building. Finally, the control rooms and the administrative spaces can be found on the first floor.

It's a building whose industrial or naval image evokes the old hospital ship, Gil Eannes, which can be found moored in the town's port, serving as a museum ship.

GIL EANNES
CALVÁRIO DA VIDA
ESPOSENSE
SENHORA DO MINHO
CAMINHA

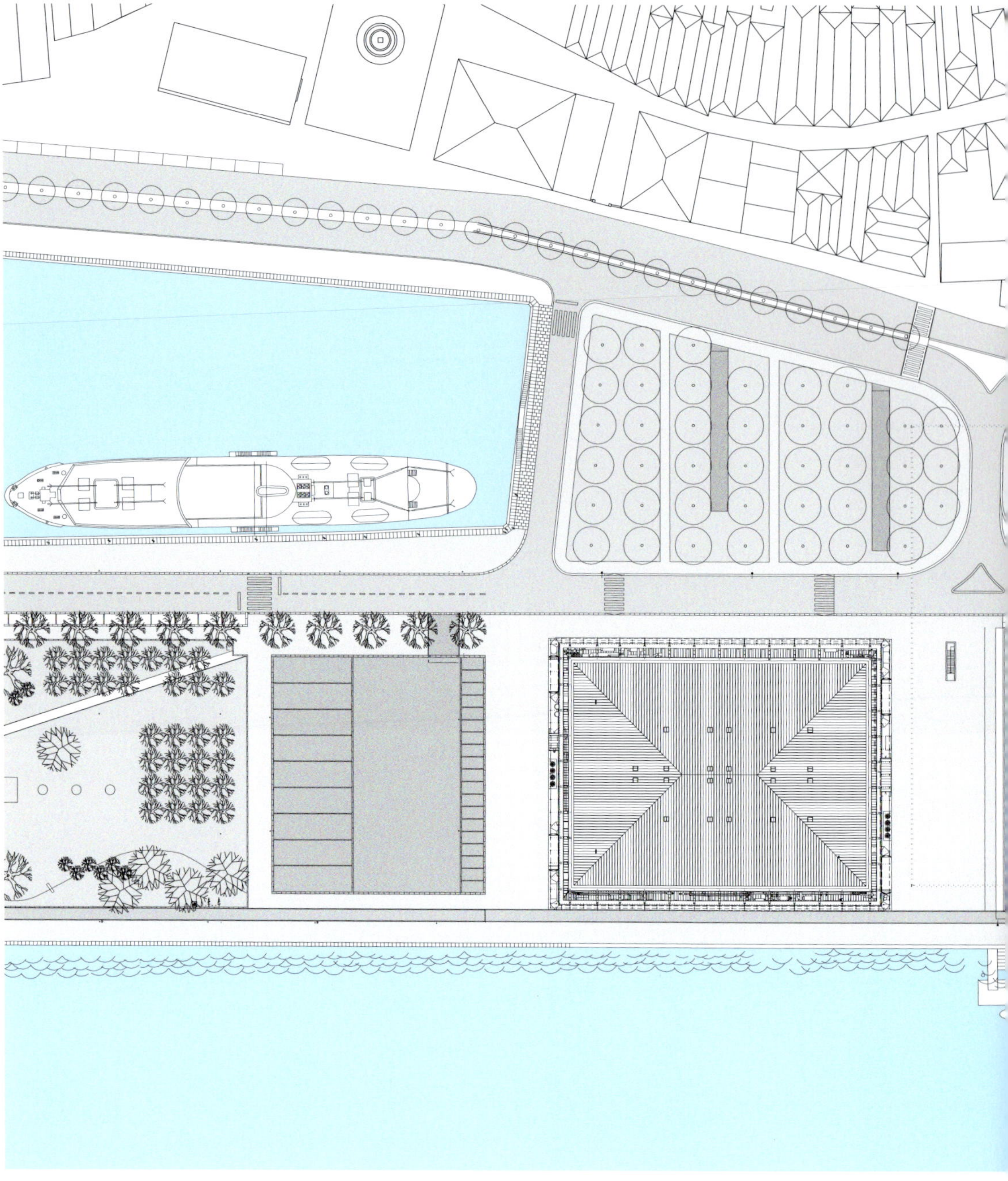

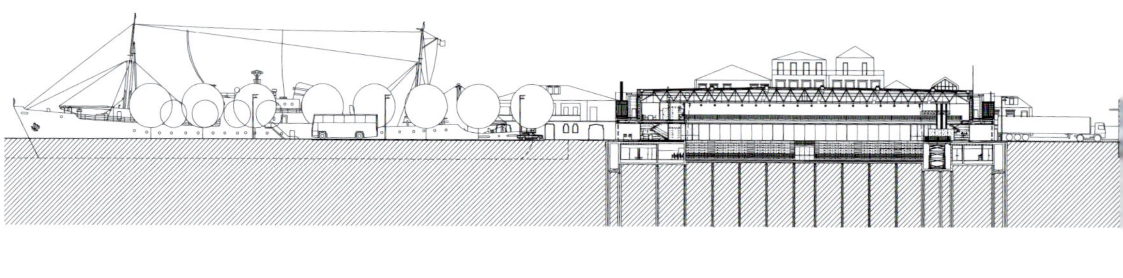

Site plan
Longitudinal section

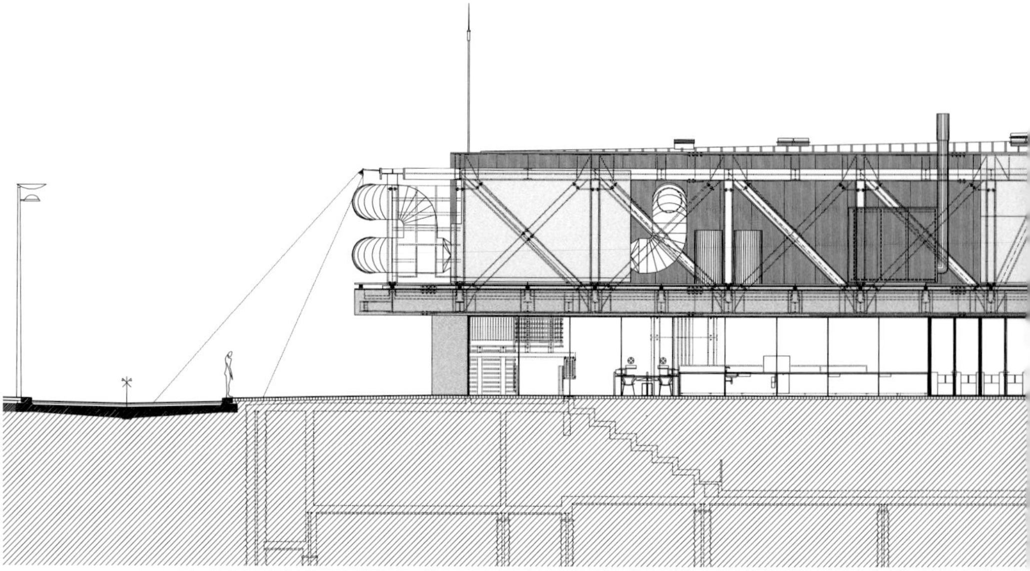

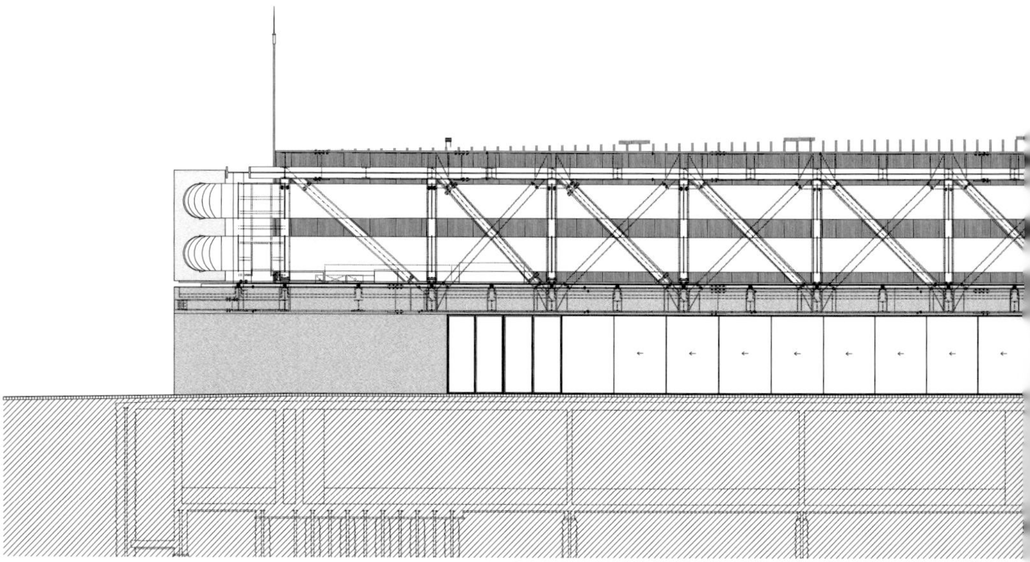

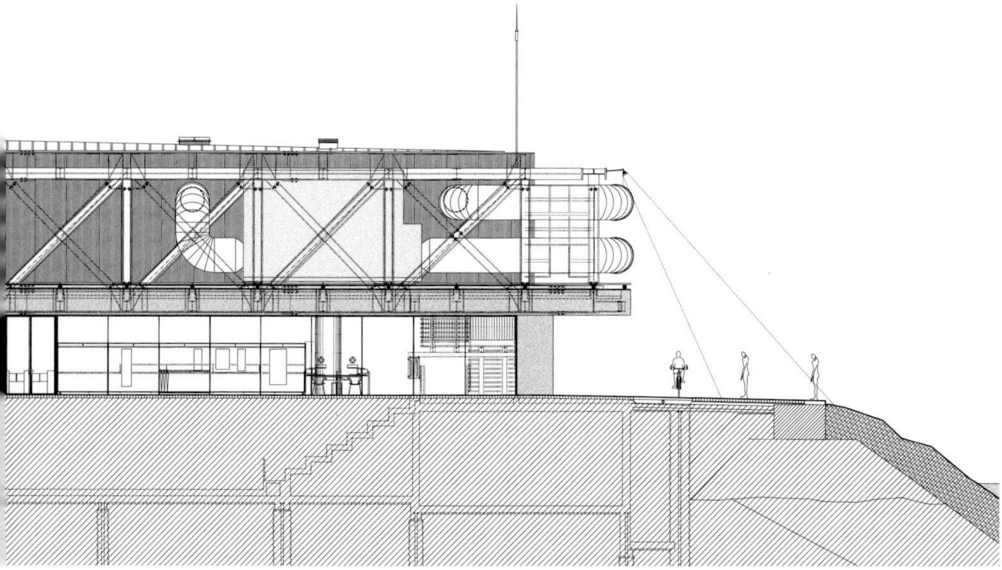

West elevation
North elevation

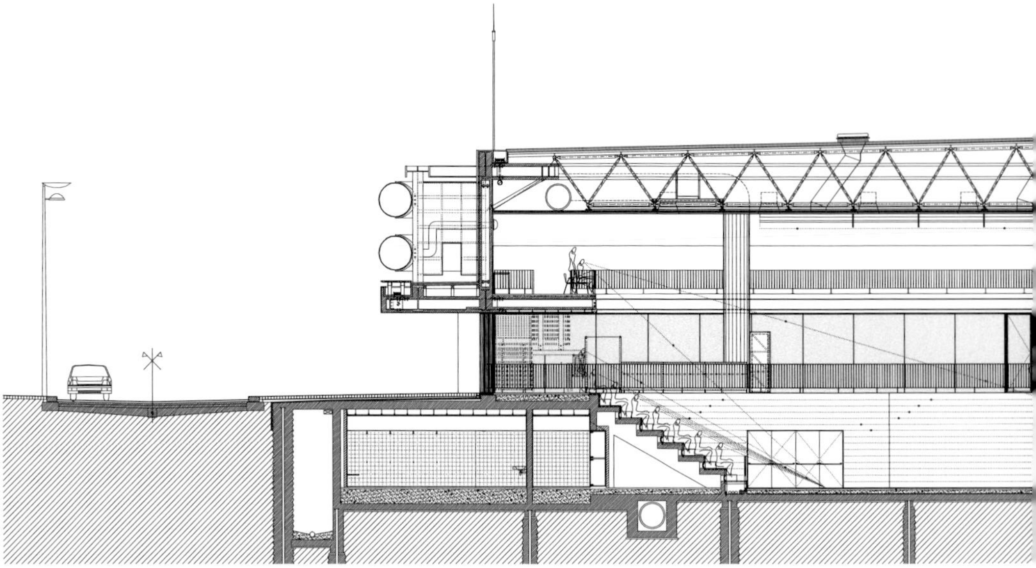

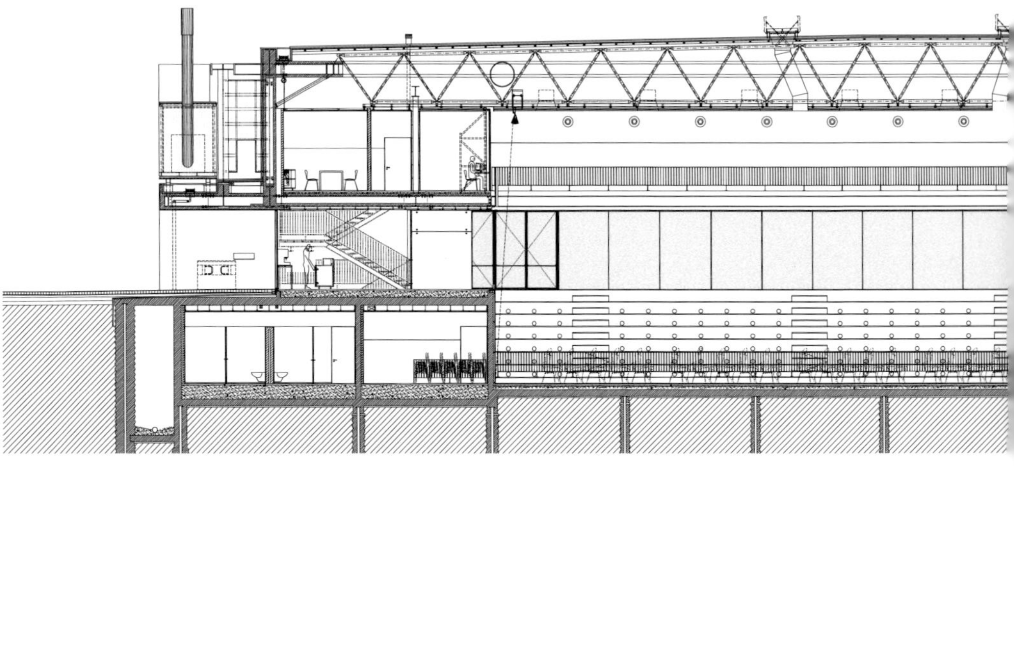

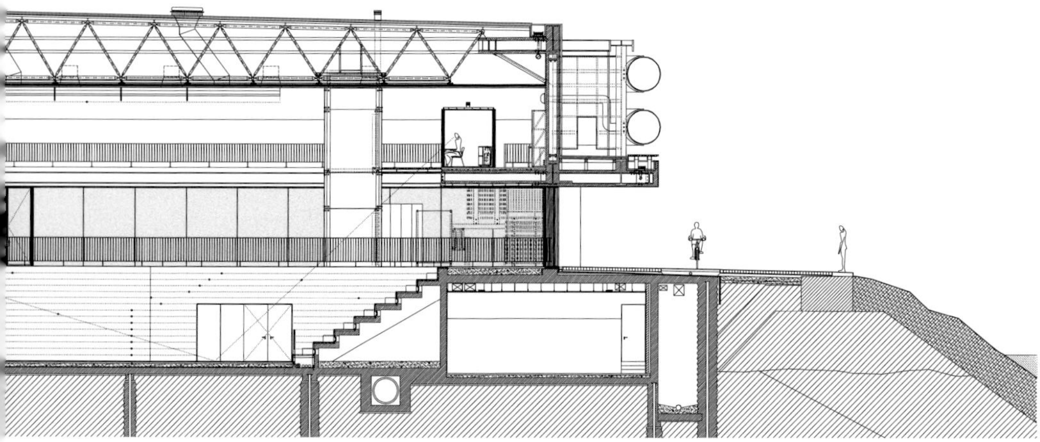

Transversal section
Longitudinal section

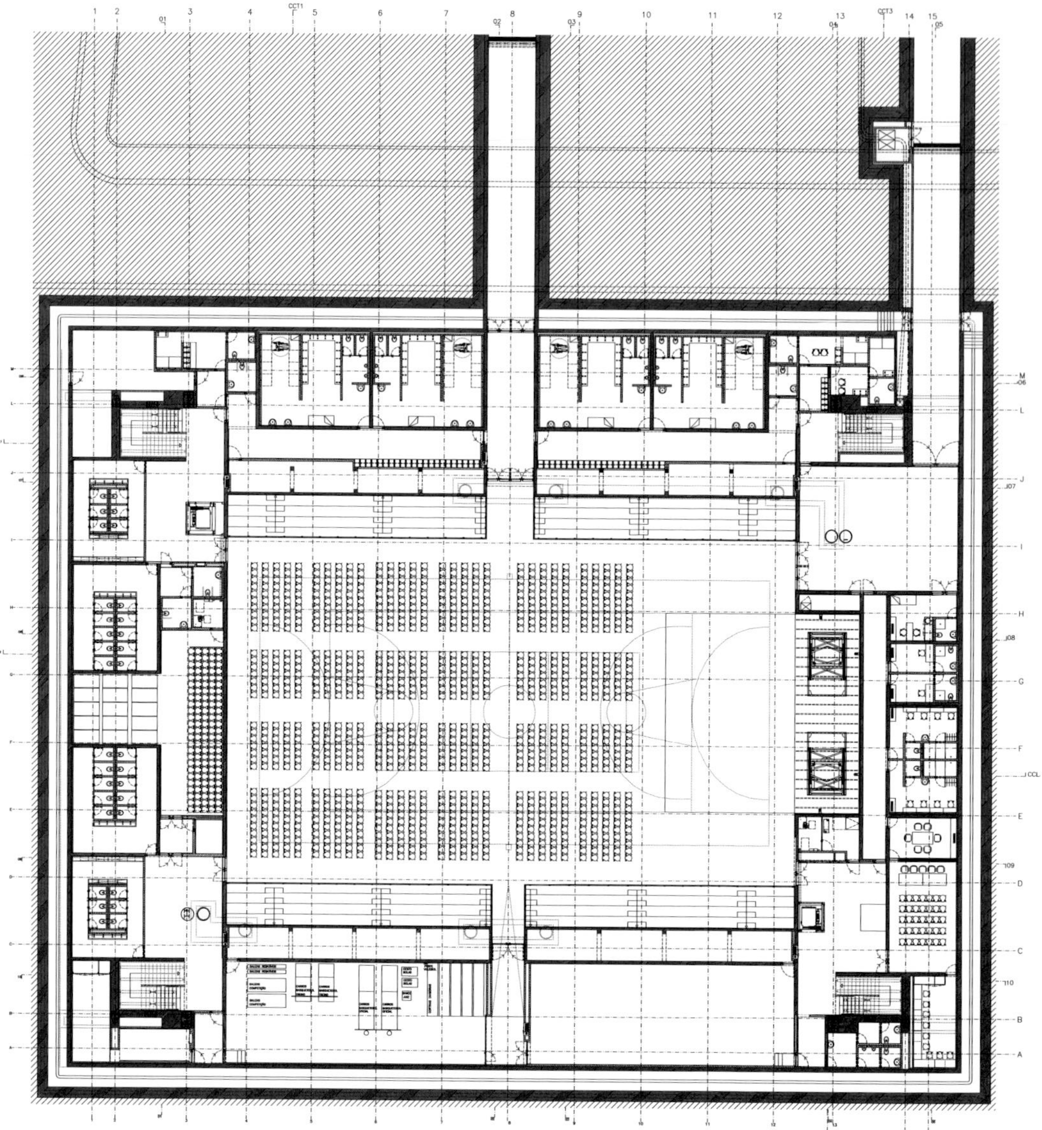

Level -1

Level 0

Level 1

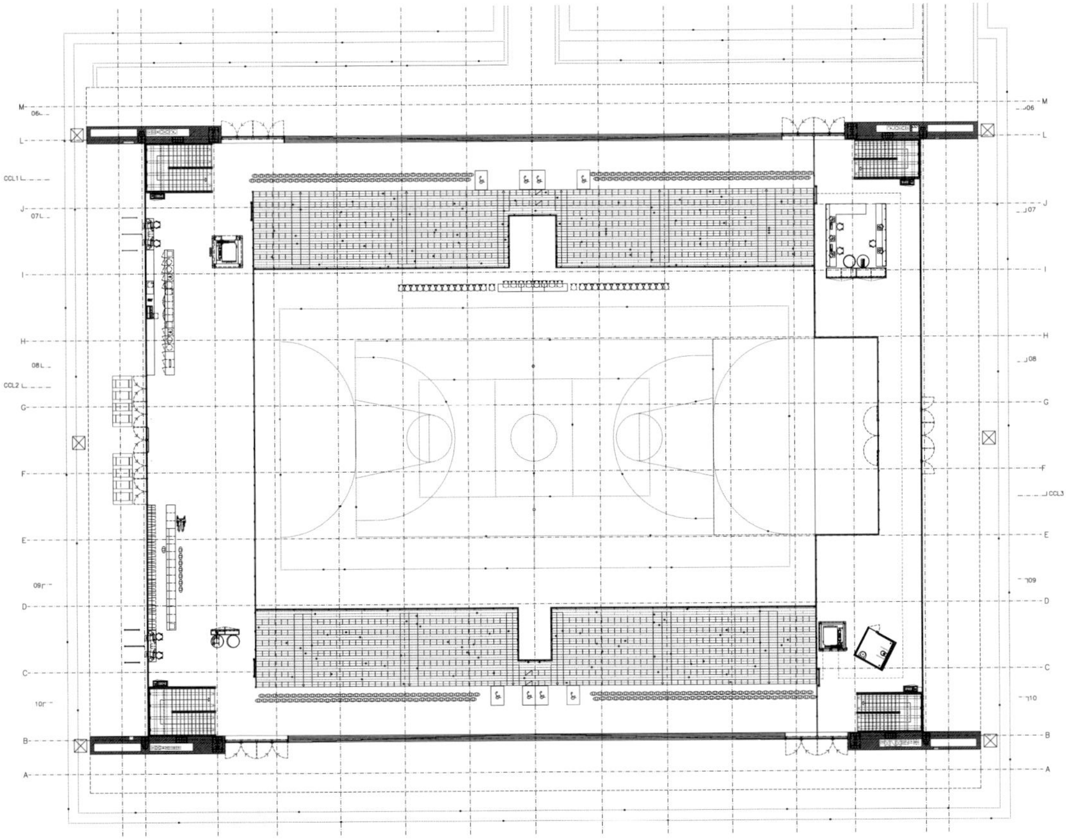

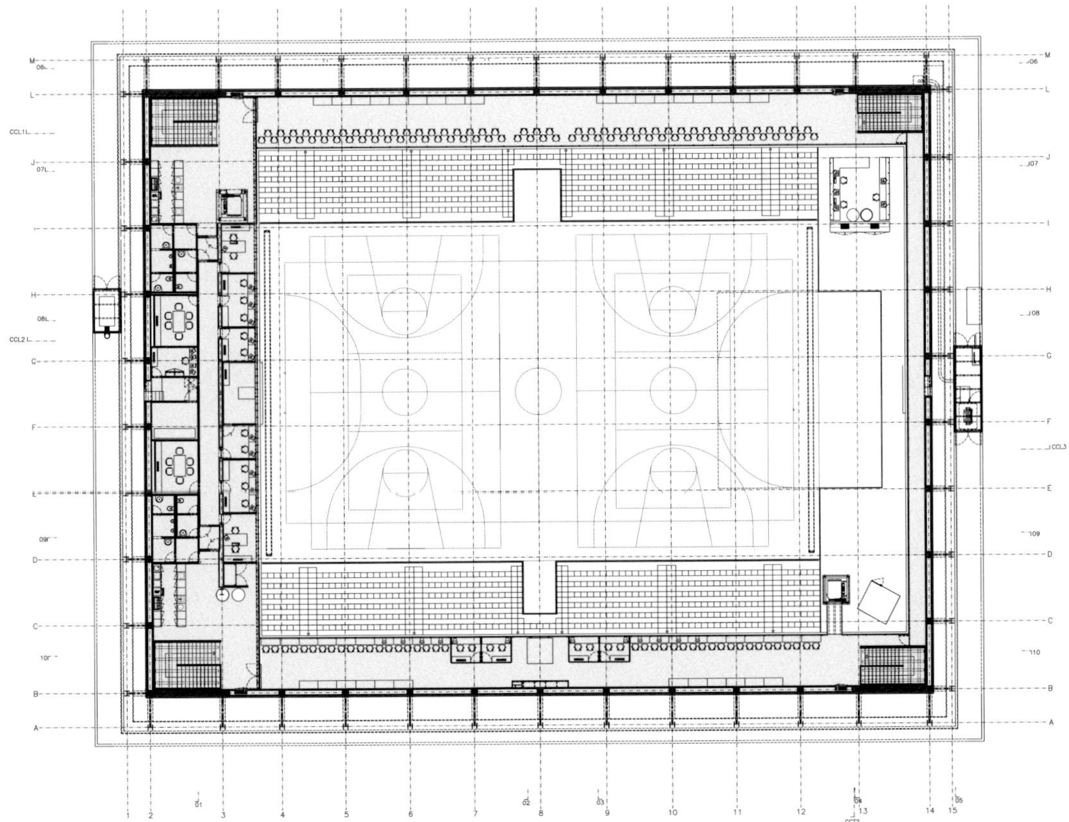

1 Souto de Moura Multipurpose pavilion

Power plant

efacec

ɔwer Plant for the Foz
a Dam. Installations,
arehouses, control
d office buildings.
ijó, Douro, Portugal
ɔ11–2018

The main concern of the project was to minimize the visual impact of the dam, achieve the greatest possible integration and eliminate the character of the building in this almost entirely underground construction, which adopts forms and materials characteristic of the region; aiming to present itself as a "machine" placed in the landscape. The whole project has sought to minimize the morphological alterations of the slopes, to compact the construction by reducing the exposed volume of the works and their visual impact.

At the base of the mountain a technical building of the plant is located, built on terraces and covered with topsoil to give continuity and finish to the cut made. This building is only visible via some concrete caissons with access and ventilation exits. A concrete platform covers the large buried atrium and the wells where the reversible turbine-pumping systems are located. On the platform there is a gantry crane, and the transformers... those elements have to be placed outdoors, positioned in the most condensed way possible. To make this 36 m wide platform, it was necessary to make a 45° cut of the mountain. To get the most natural final shape possible, the rock was cut and fixed with an almost imperceptible metallic net, avoiding the use of concrete walls for containment. On this slope olive trees will be planted to create continuity with the nearby lands.

The social building is buried under the main platform, between the two cylinders that contain the auxiliary engines; from the outside, only a line of 25 m with one meter in height to give light and ventilation to the program is visible. Inside are the control, centre meeting rooms, changing rooms, services...

A glass box for the observation post and an inverted cone-shaped water tank, made of concrete, contrast with the natural richness of the surroundings.

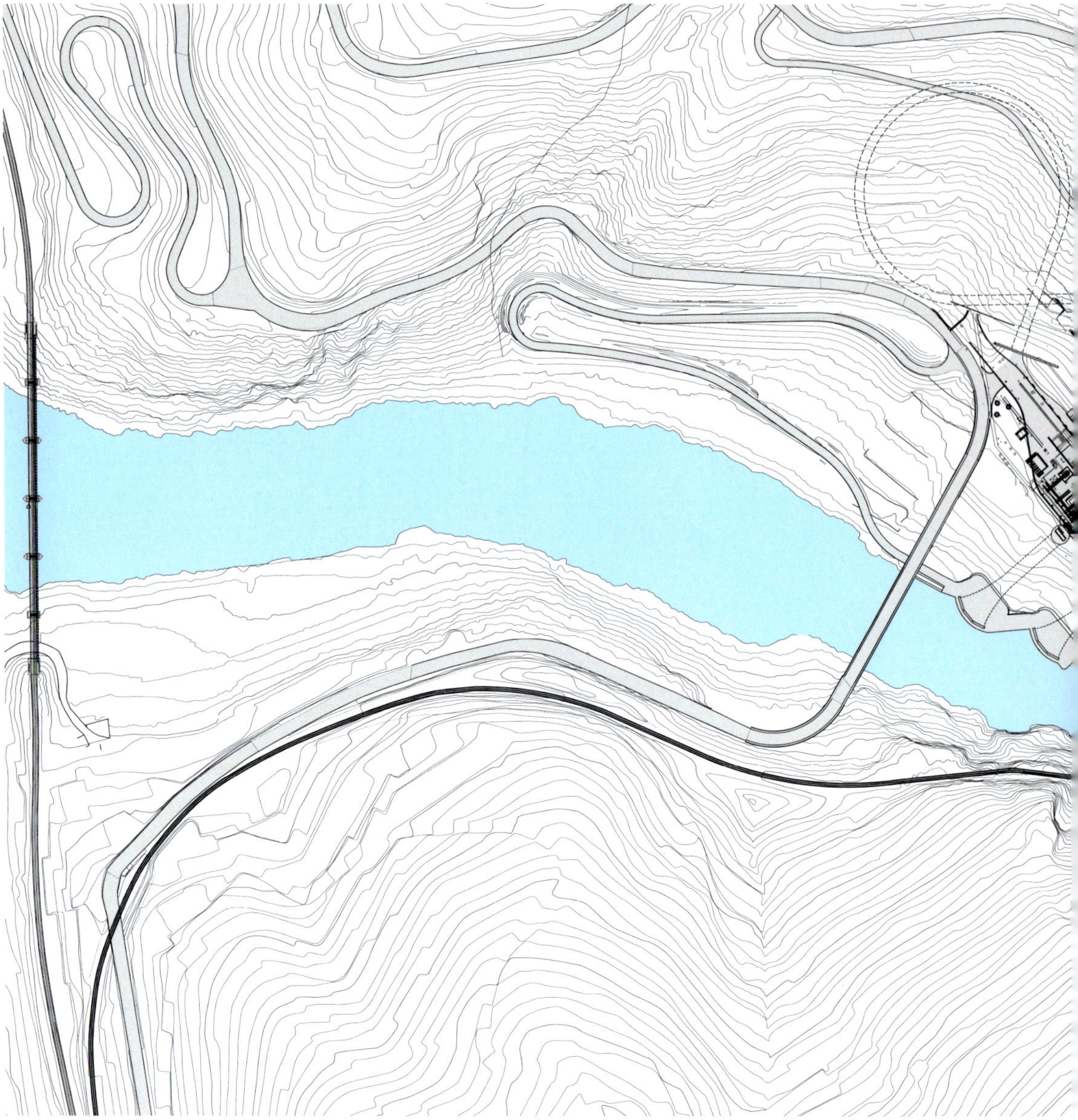

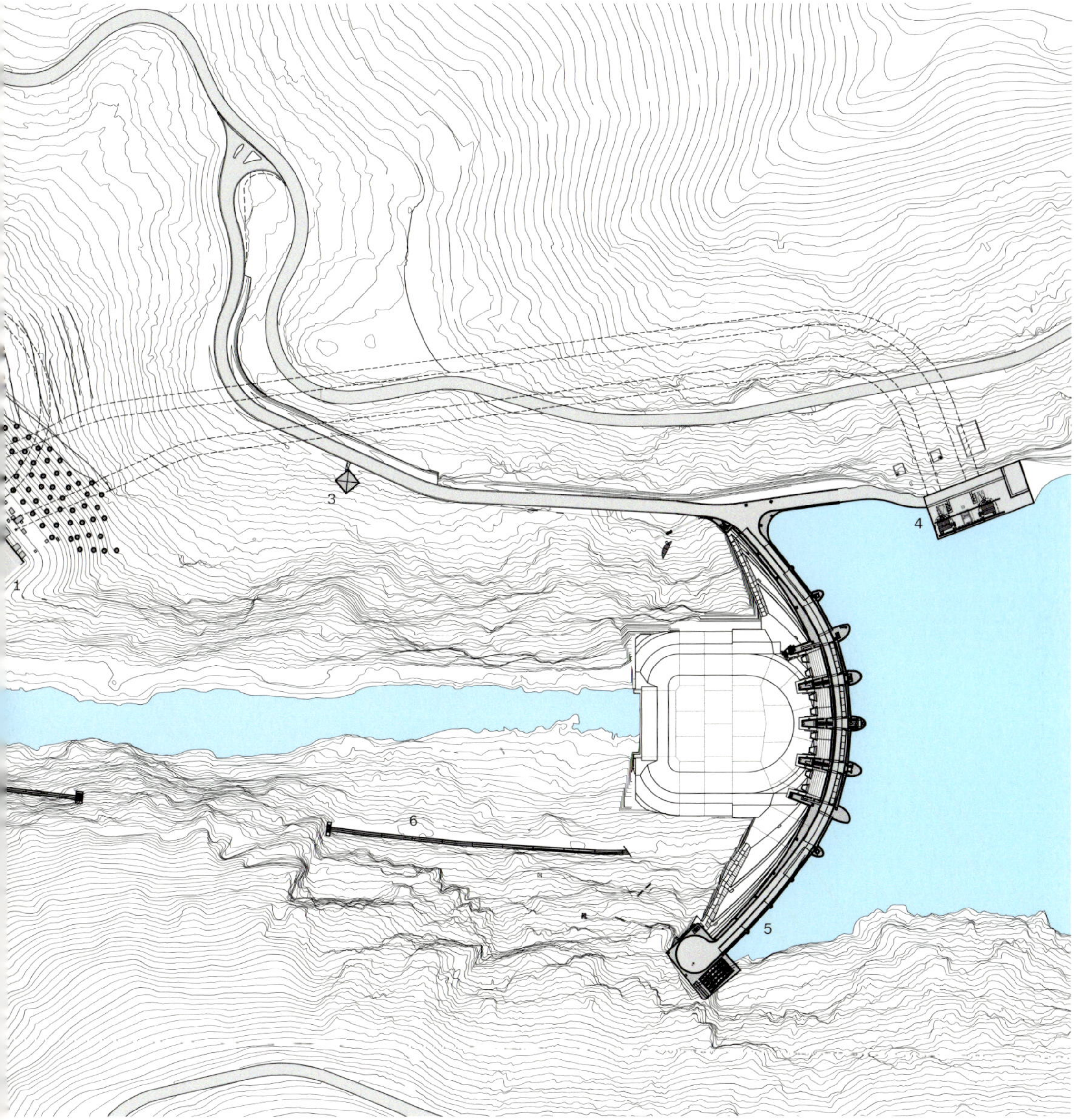

1. Hydroelectric power station
2. Water tank
3. Information and control station
4. Water supply
5. Dam
6. Rail track

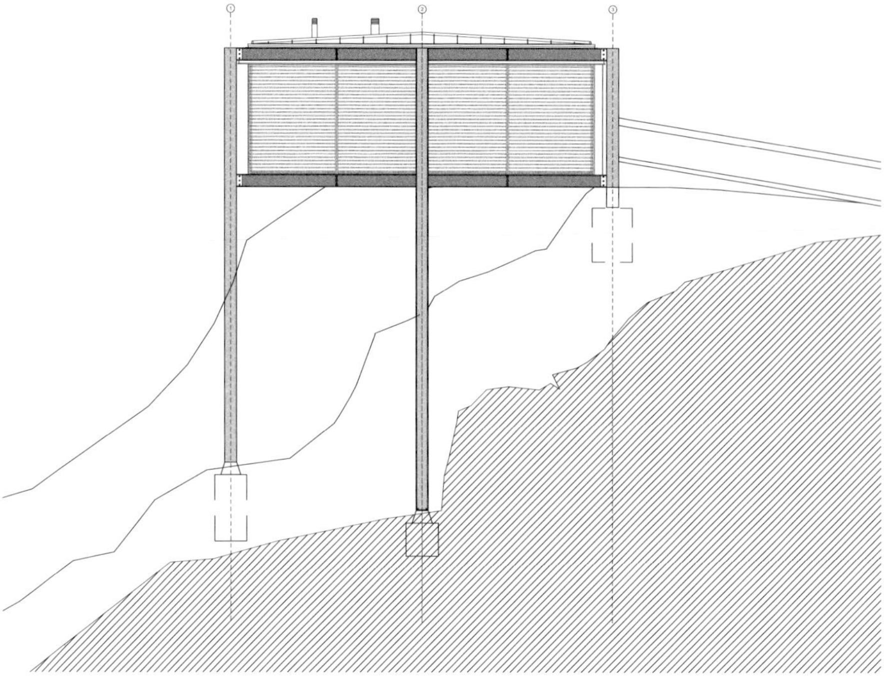

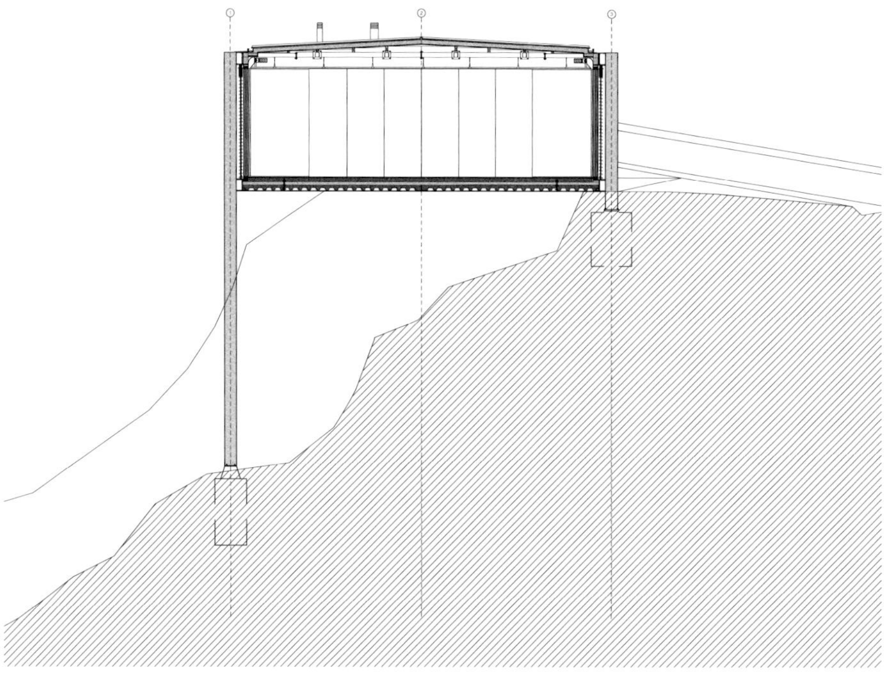

Information and control point. Sections

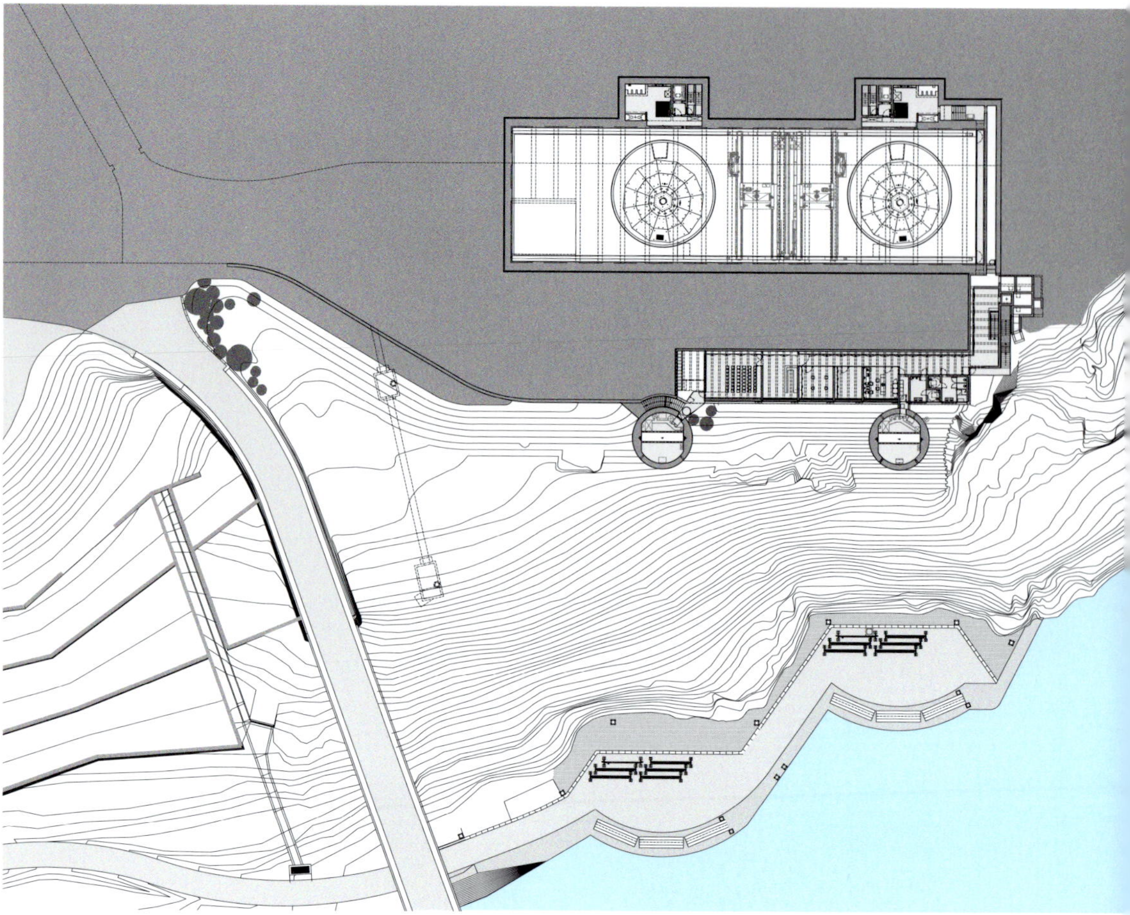

Atrium and office level

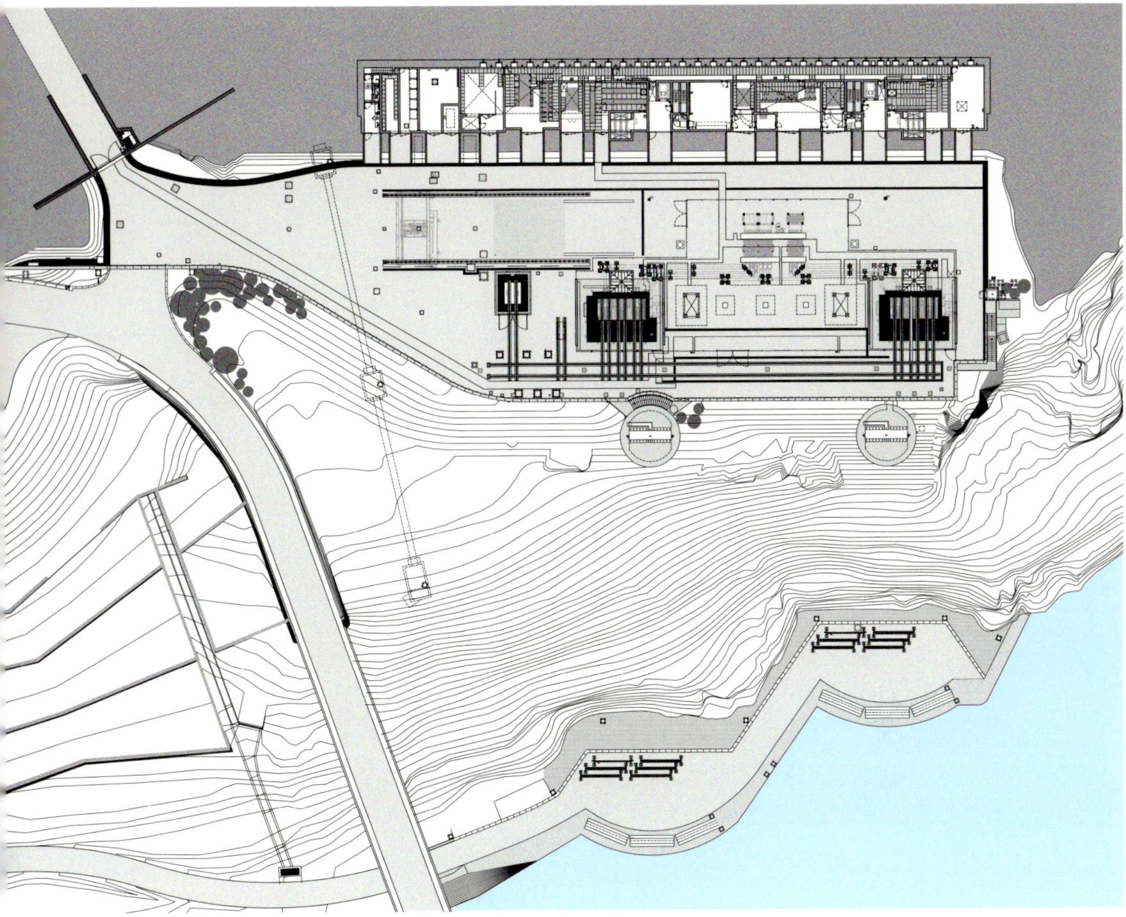

Entrance level

efacec

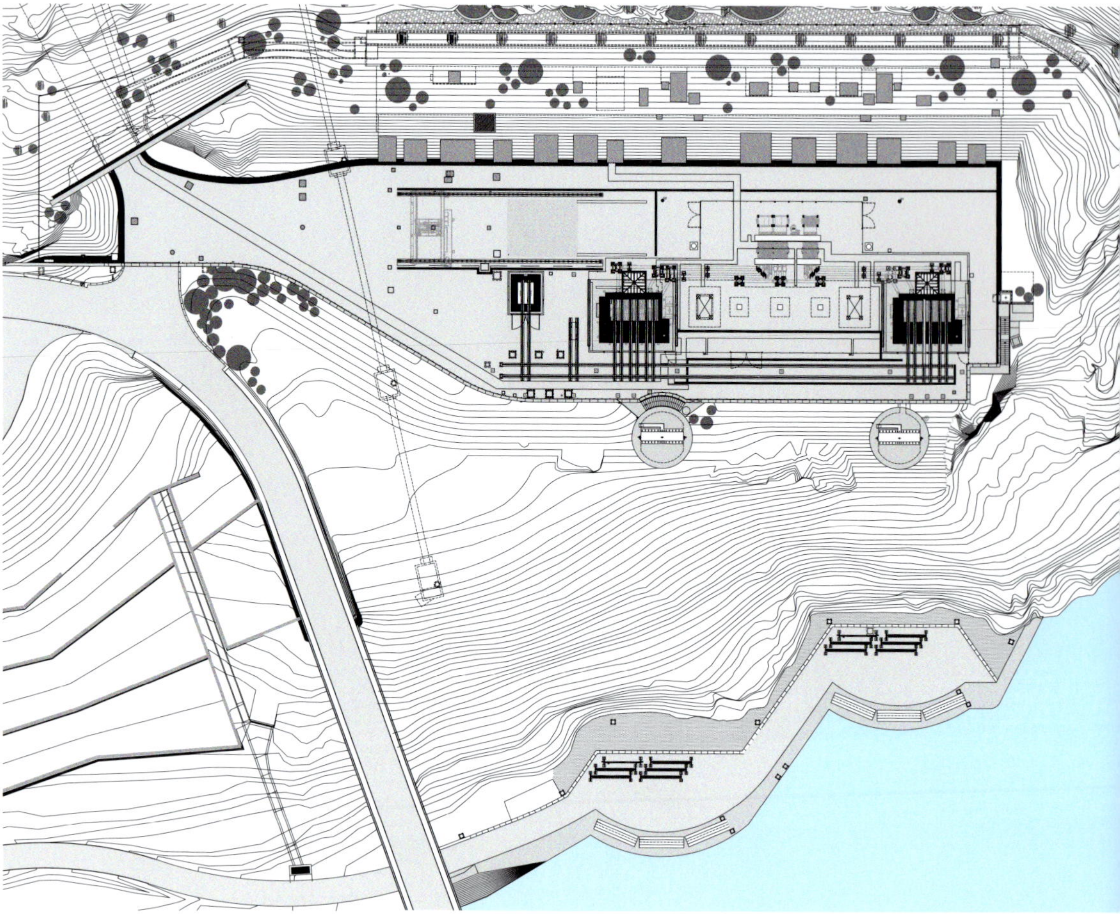

Roof level

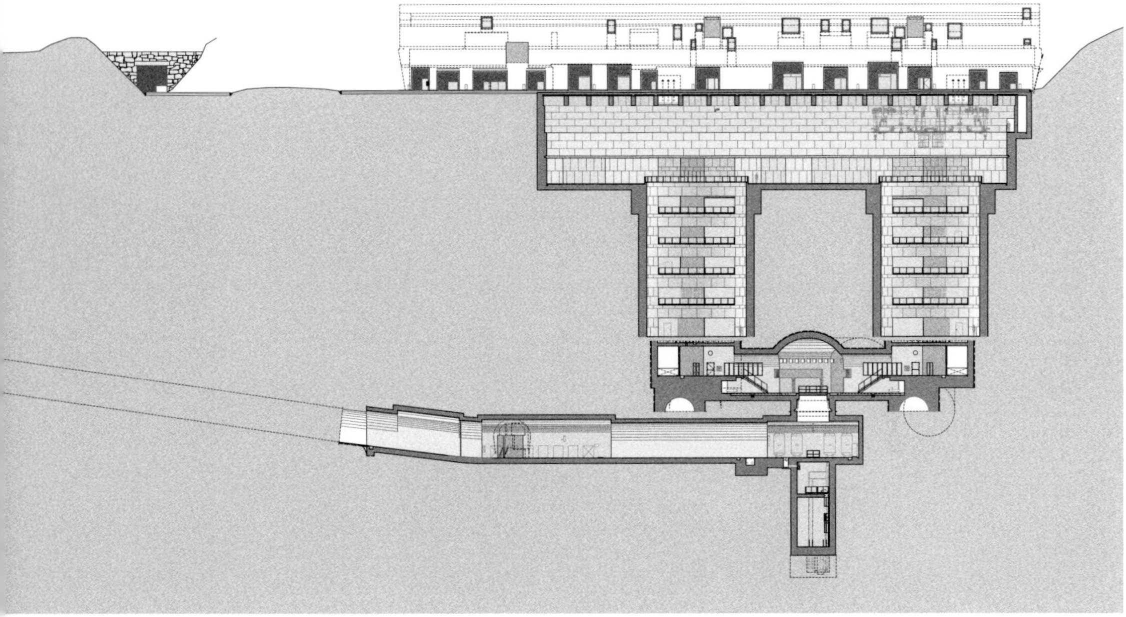

1 Souto de Moura Power plant Longitudinal section

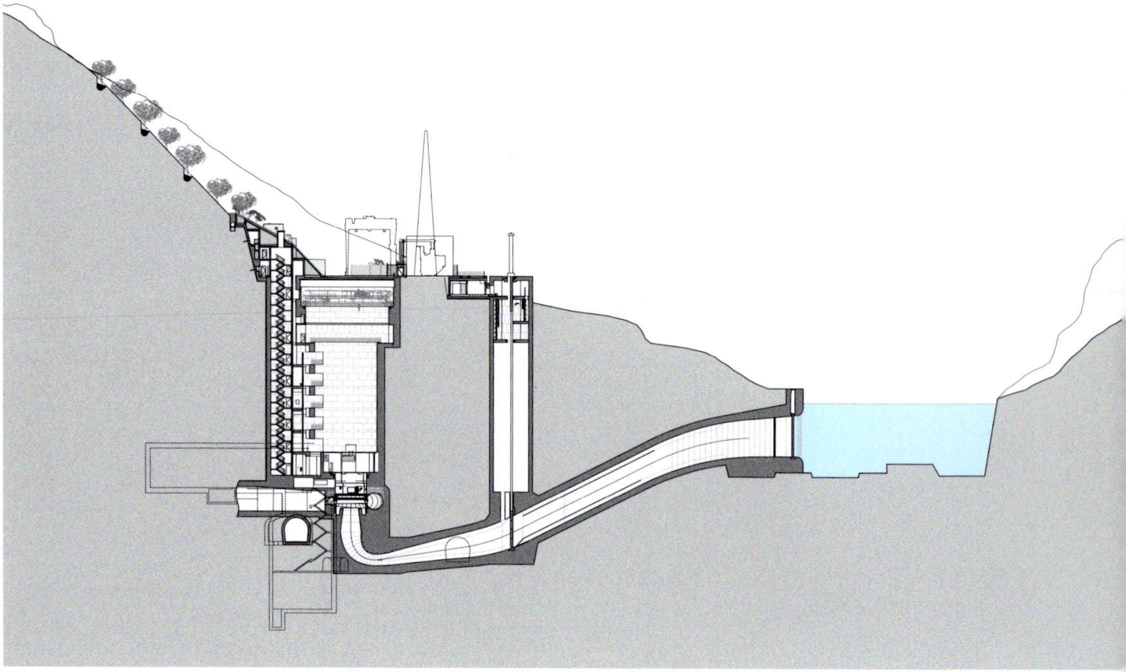

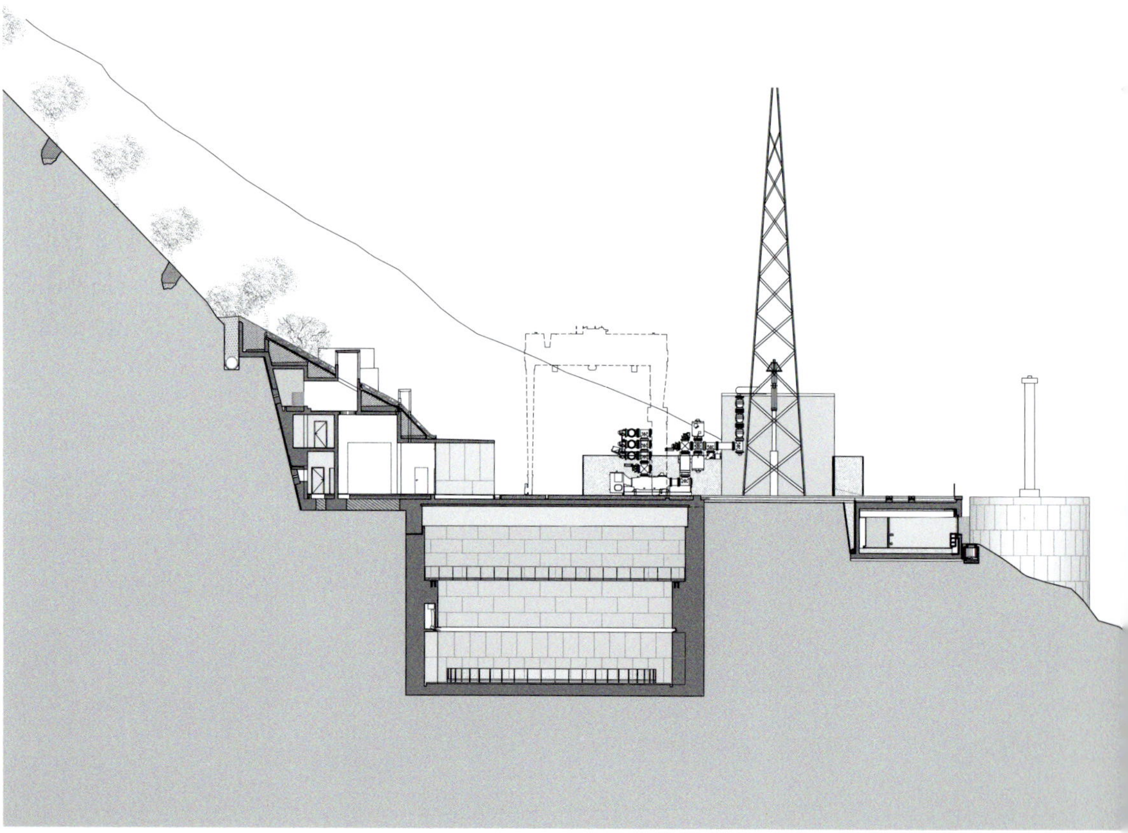

7 Souto de Moura Power plant

150/25 t. (Máx. 150 t.)
OF: 49.689 CE-2014
efacec

House in Quinta do Lago

lteration and extension f the House in Quinta o Lago (1984–1989). lgarve, Portugal 015–2017

This is a project with two stages, the first occured in 1984–1989 when this house was designed and built for holidays in the Algarve, next to a golf course. With very clear rules, imposed by urbanization, the house emerged as a parallelepiped supported on the grass.

The initial project was inspired by a merge of popular Southern Portuguese architecture and that of some Chinese houses (the project was carried out in Macau). It is not unlike the previous works of Souto and contains references to the work of Le Corbusier.

Three decades later, the new owner wants to increase its size with a larger kitchen, a more spacious living room, with a dining room, an independent suite and space to store at least four cars.

In order to respond to the new conditions and the obligation to preserve the building, the project increases the volume while retaining all the features, “stretching” the building and achieving a proportion in the lightest of ensembles. The original inspiration for the building is maintained. Part of the program goes underground and so cars and storage areas are located in a basement which is accessed via an elevator, so that their presence disappears when they are not in use.

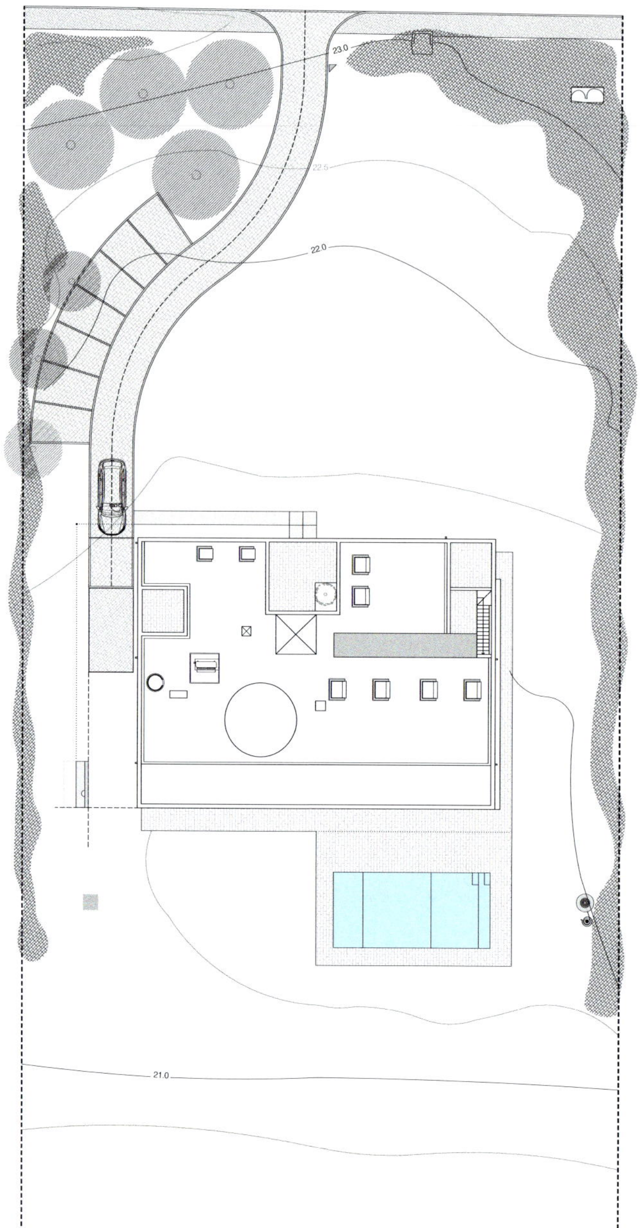

Site plan

1 Souto de Moura House in Quinta do Lago

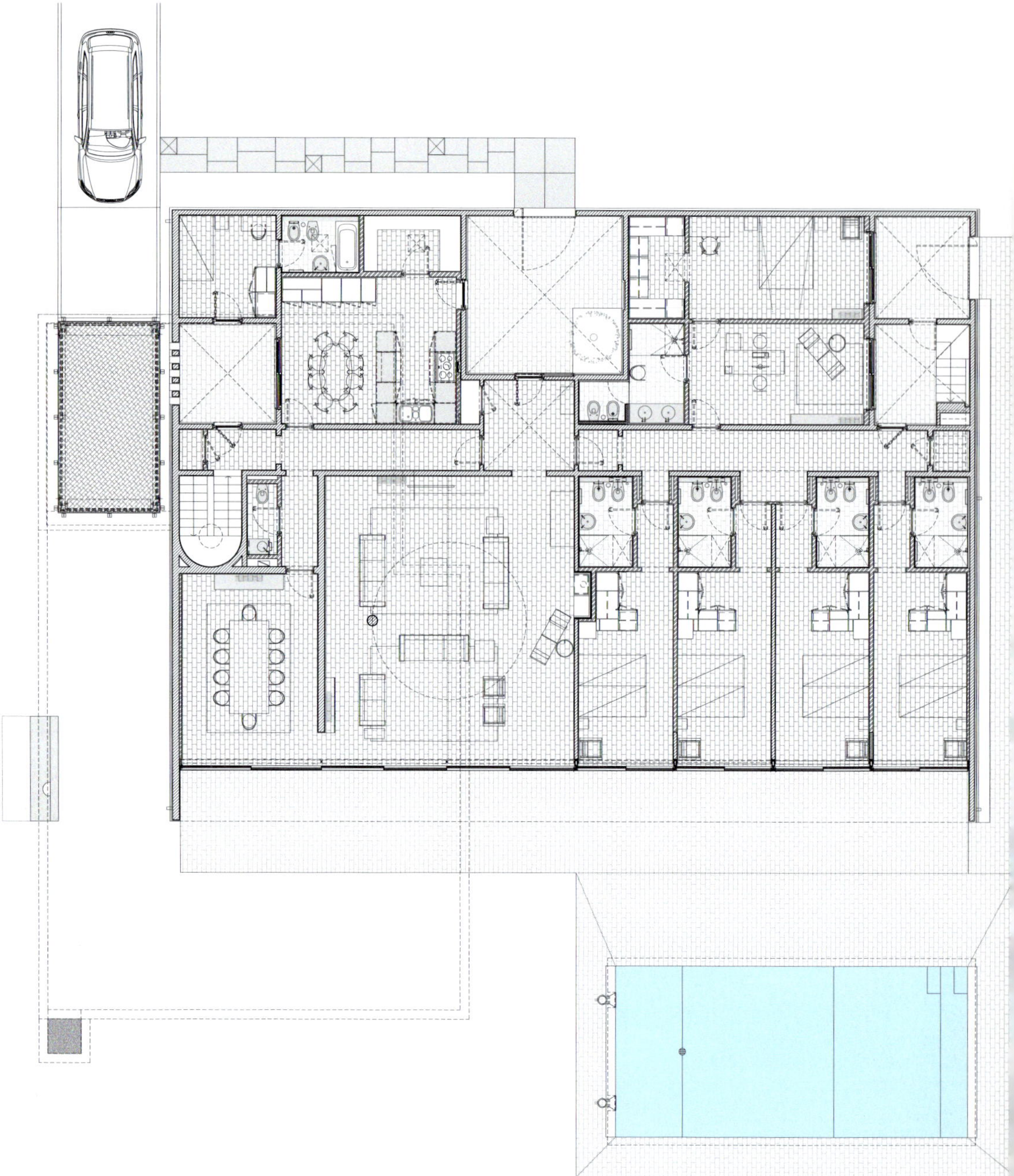

Ground floor

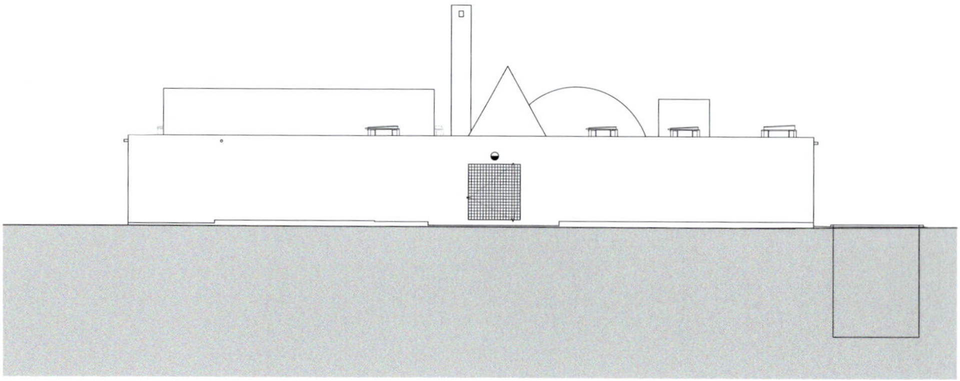

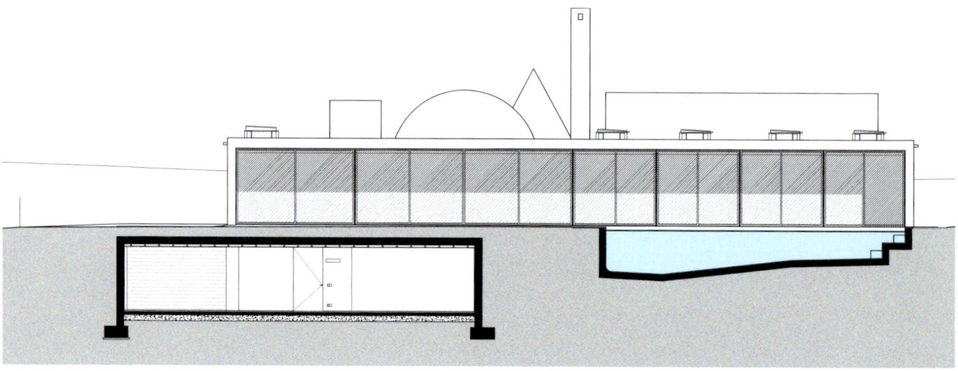

South east elevation
South west elevation

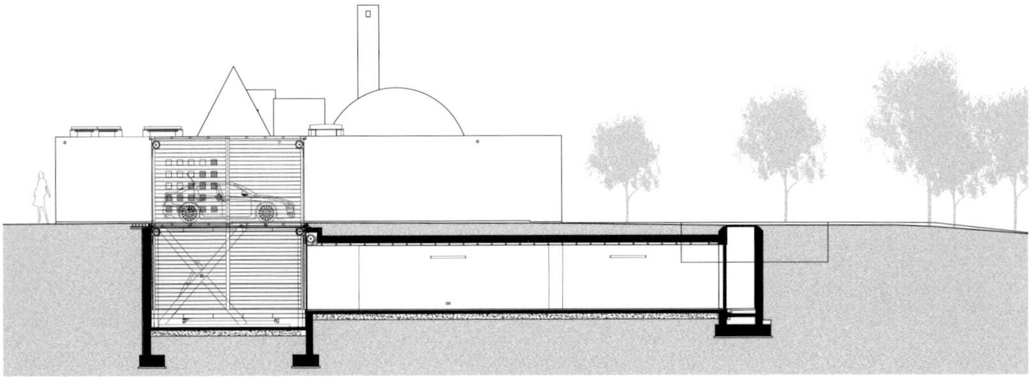

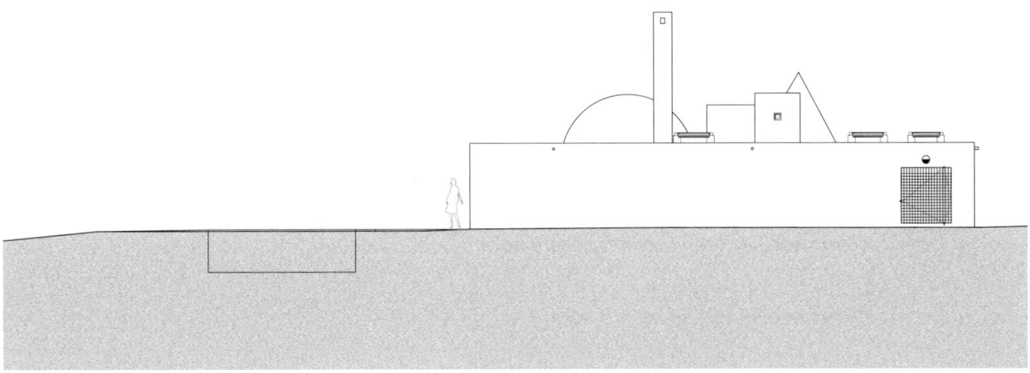

North east elevation
North west elevation

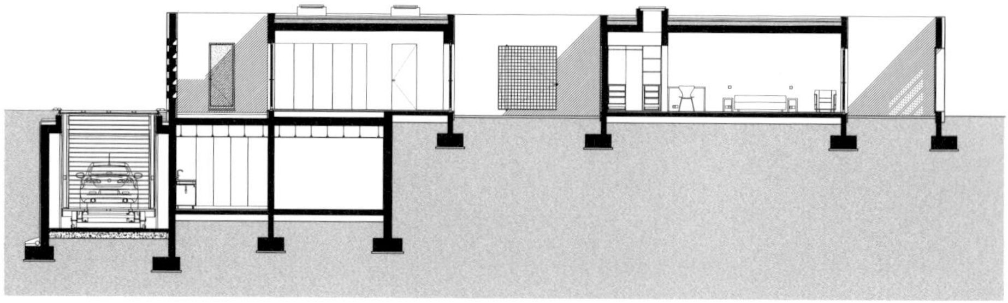

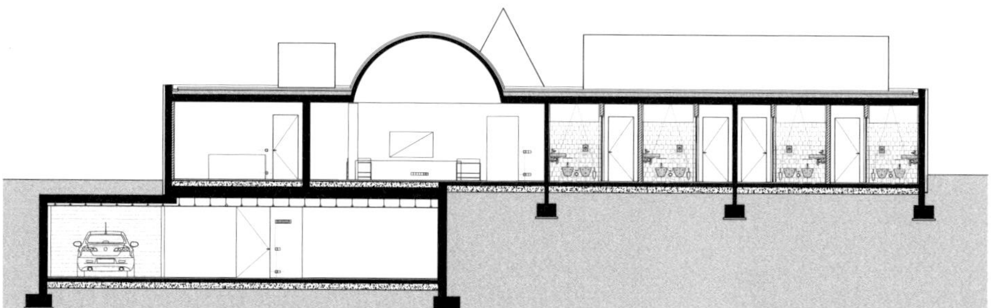

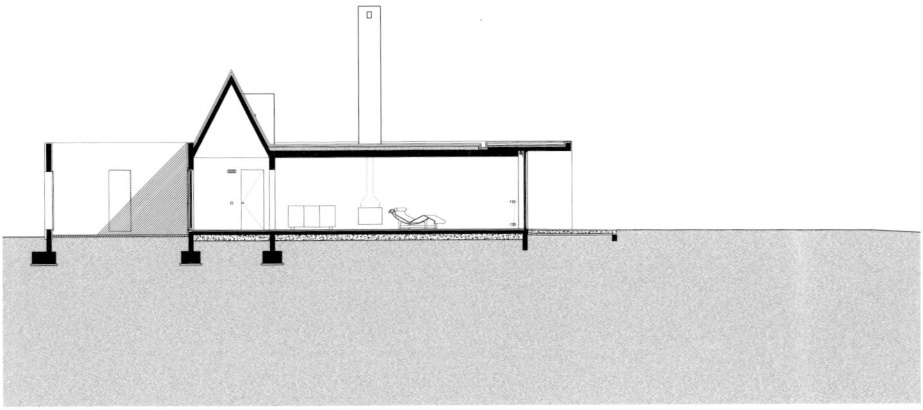

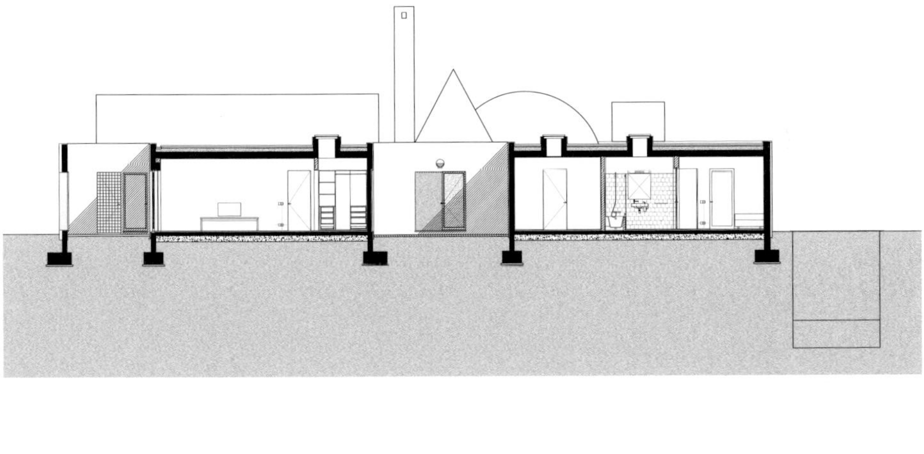

A Caida

ntervention of the
xisting buildings in
uinta da Caida-Arcas.
acedo de Cavaleiros,
ortugal
009-2019

A Caida was a small abandoned nucleus of five buildings in a considerable state of degradation. With more uniform characteristics in the main ensemble of four buildings, and differentiated by the isolated construction of an old cattle farm. All of them have recognisable characteristics of different moments of an anonymous architecture.

Conserving everything that was built, a new building has been added to increase the accomodation units and achieve economic viability for the proposal. This new building has been imagined as another stone wall, placed to solve a change in terrain height and to minimise the destruction of the plant lining with its positioning. Three of the buildings contain accommodation, close to a service building which will also serve as a reception. The isolated cattle farm is used as a home for the caretakers of the buildings and the agricultural holding.

The existing layout has been preserved adopting traditional construction methods that are characteristic of this zone. The existing materials have been maintained and unity has been sought by covering all the walls with a waterproof protection, and the isolated construction of the cattle farm has been improved by the most careful use of brick possible.

A consolidation of walls, new paving of a great thickness, adequate opening of gaps, chimneys designed from a plastic vision of the ensemble–these are some of the key points of the project that has always looked at what existed in the nearest villages and has improved it through very simple operations focused on details, thickness and materials.

A Caida is a delicate operation that eliminates the presence of a recognisable author and which contains a serious look towards necessary intervention in all that has been left by the instability and immediacy in the majority of Portugal's rural territory.

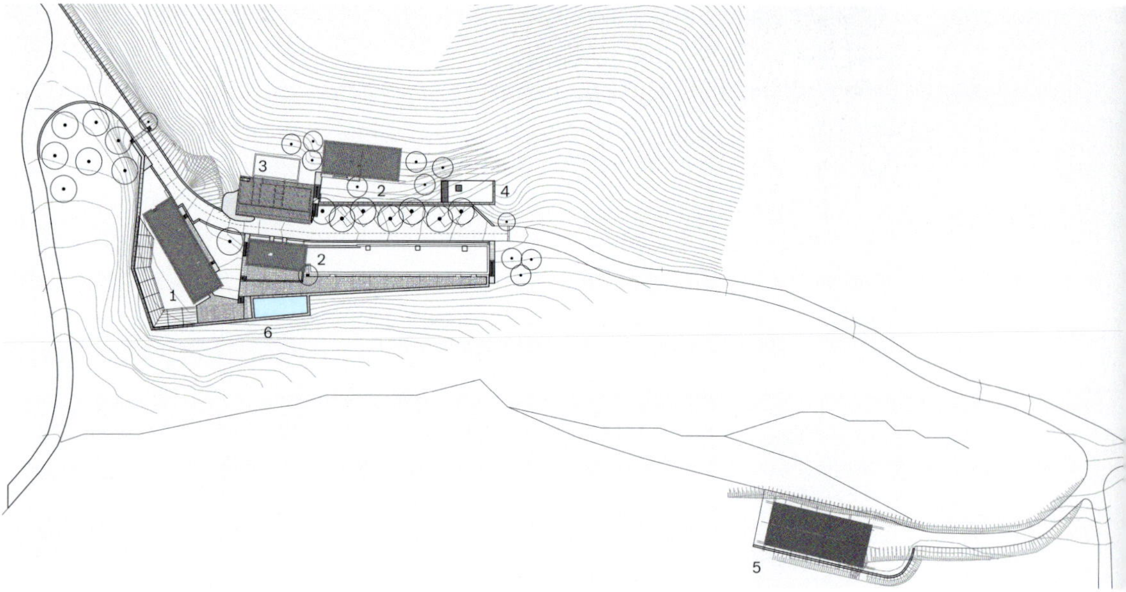

1. Restaurant
2. Apartments
3. Reception
4. Technical area
5. Caretakers' house
6. Pool

Site plan

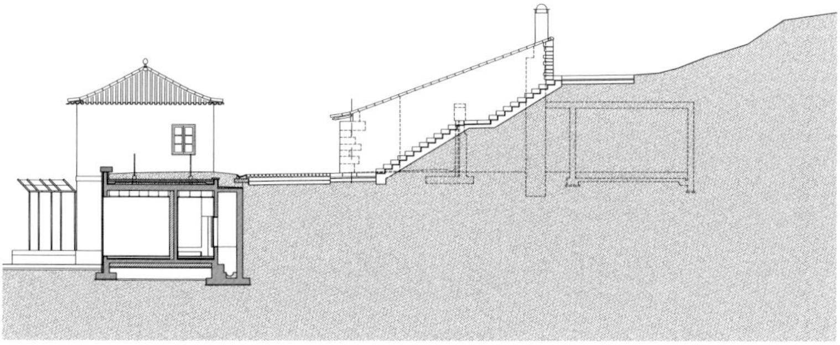

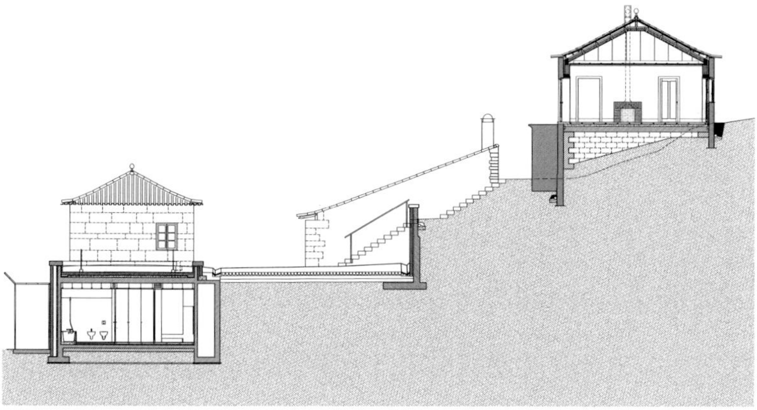

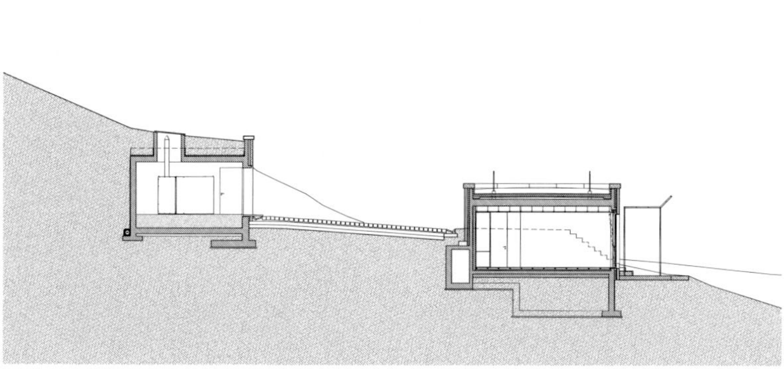

Pedro Cabrita Reis

Carlos Quintáns

I am the revolution

‹rt light installation
ı Restaurant Oficina.
'orto. 2016

ınstallation for the
'014 Venice Biennale

Pedro Cabrita arrives at his workshop with the remains of something burned that he has found on the street. Some metallic pieces stick out in an ensemble that at one point must have been fluid, and that had taken on the shape of the ground on which it had been leaning and of the discontinuity of what could have fallen while burning. An informative piece that has gained circumstantially a "suitable" form so that it may be used at any time in the work of Cabrita. An object that is dropped near many others that have already been used: doors, windows, glass, chairs... Everything perfectly ordered.

The Cabrita workshop is an old warehouse inside a large building. The windows that face the interior of this complex allow you to see an enormous area where many of his works coexist behind a door that reads "a revolução sou eu" (I am the revolution). The floor above houses the area where the pieces are prepared and processed and a slightly elevated office. On a higher floor is the house which is reached by passing a completely white structure, with a staircase, which separates it from the work area. The house allows for a free longitudinal view as in the other two floors, with huge spaces and wonderful furniture ready to be used or simply contemplated.

We begin the conversation in his office, in front of some of his books (the others are kept in his house near Tavira). Every so often, some will be thrown away in order to filter them down and preserve only those that are relevant to his work. Books that support him in the knowledge he has of himself. He confesses that this “cleaning” comes from someone who likes to cast his eyes on the future and who prefers to have a fragile memory.

He has no problems working with the people who come to see him. The workshop is a meeting place, a place where they become closer: some speak, others create… Here there is no silence, silence is interior. There is no rejection. His workshop is a place of convergence, a factory of thought in which there are no models.

In the year 2021, he hopes that his foundation can be inaugurated with a project by Eduardo Souto de Moura, although it is too early to talk about it. He has only worked with Eduardo on the crematorium in Cortrique, in Belgium, in the building for Novartis in Basel and in the exhibition *D'après Fibonacci e as coisas lá fora* (According to Fibonacci and things out there) by Jorge Pinheiro in the Serralves Foundation. They meet, they observe, they talk, they don't need more. It is not a continuous relationship, but when they meet he has the feeling of continuing their last conversation, theirs is an intense relationship of

project and thought.
For Pedro, Eduardo is a unique person of clear thought; with a work that lives by itself. He is interested in Eduardo as a man who thinks, as a philosopher, a poet, with whom he has an elective affinity, going back to Kant. Pedro finds the way that Eduardo looks at the world intriguing –it's a look that interrogates, and Pedro is also interested in Eduardo's drawings with which he wants to transform the world.

Pedro speaks forcefully, without hesitation, in an emphatic manner. It is so clear that it seems that he has prepared his conversation so that it can be literally transcribed.

Cabrita's work is also very clear and there is a perception that he has a very similar way of looking at things to an architect, but in reality architecture does not interest him. He is interested in the act of construction. The programs of the two disciplines are different, with points of contact and a thought that is coincidental.

The architect, when looking at the context, observes it in the same way in which the artist looks at the thought in which he finds himself. Architecture is an intellectual device that has to do with the political management of space, whether private or public. Architecture is the response of humanity to the act of living together–to design the policy of

Eduardo & Gabita
21.12
@ Papaçada, Lisboa

coexistence, that is what interests the architect.
An artist does not have to answer a question, a proposal based on reality; born from an imagination that emerges from reality. There is no art out of reality. There is no art outside of critical thinking.

Abstract art is as abstract as a self-portrait of the fifteenth or sixteenth century. There is no abstract art, there are responses to stimuli, to circumstances in historical, philosophical, poetical, political contexts, of a narrative nature, more abstract or more philosophical. Cabrita as an artist is concerned about the philosophical anthropology of the relationship between the individual and nature: the act of placing a stone on another stone and thereby building a territory.

Humanity constructs its own nature in terms of the human species, on the nature found that serves as territory of occupation. Art seeks to imagine and reproduce the different possibilities of the individual's relationship with their natural context, understanding that it can also change the perception that men have of everything around them and even of themselves.

He does not find it interesting to claim an authorship, he prefers to talk about searching for a statute for each one of his pieces, a position of curiosity, and with that build a new narrative.

The conversation with Pedro Cabrita is long and intense, that of someone who does not hide his thoughts and from whom a contagious vitality springs.

Something more than a text was necessary and Pedro managed to get an image of his latest work printed in the restaurant. On it, he draws two chimneys with pencil, to which he adds with his hand the remainder of the red wine from the dinner. Eduardo & Cabrita.

Continuity, corners and collage in the architecture of Souto de Moura

Santiago de Molina

Thirty thousand people cheered each time Sporting Clube de Braga entered the field. The crowd cheered and the stadium, popularly known amongst the fans as "A Pedreira" (The Quarry), resounds like another huge spectator, due to the echo that is produced by the monumental cut stone of the mountain nearby.

Undoubtedly this stone wall will remain oblivious to the result of the current sporting event, as will the blind, concrete stadium that embraces it. However, the crowd will slowly leave that space and go back to the city, firstly by making their way down the stands, then the thousands of interior stairs, walking between the ribs of this grand, hollow, concrete animal, either happy or deflated depending on the game's ever uncertain result. The stadium, uncompromisingly hardy, appears silent and colossal, and it will be an empty space waiting for new event for another week. But, maybe this numbness is not what it seems. Because the stadium lives within a rhythmic system of another order, of another time, able to combine weekly matches with the mineral eternity of the rock upon which it rests.

If a thorough analysis of the construction of the Municipal Stadium of Braga were to be carried out, it would be impossible to overlook how a sense of time outside of everyday life, similar to that described above, can be felt within it. So much so that one can say that this is a building made with stone, spectators, concrete, and that rhythmical time.

The combination of these elements is reminiscent of old Greek theatres and the spirit that spectators must have inhaled in the stands of the Epidauro or the Taormina. Even the relationship the stadium has with its landscape and how the spectacle is closed off from three different sides cannot be imagined as unlike what would have occurred 2300 years ago in places so far away as those Greek amphitheatres. Neither can one imagine the relationship between a mass of people and a monument, brutal in shape and substance, yet close to exquisite in its conception, without facing a conflict that we are perhaps not prepared to address, but that is put on the table without mitigation or half-heartedness. Is it possible that just one of these spectators, submerged in the crowd, might be able to lift themselves out of the group in order to appreciate the relentless beauty of the place he or she is in? Is the stadium capable, as work of architecture, of striking with its internal logic just one of the brains of these people that cheer on their team at the top of their lungs on a Sunday evening?

One can sense the answer. However, it remains a necessary question to ask for anyone interested in the possibilities that architecture has to alter the lives of the people who inhabit it. It is almost certain that this question must have occupied the creator of this work. The distance that

Municipal Stadium of Braga. Portugal. 2003

exists between the form of the proposed and designed architecture, the coherence, and the final construction, the significance of the work as a cultural entity and its impact on life, means perceiving an abyss that is difficult to fill. That gap between the form of architecture and life, is, I think, the great theme which is being offered and update here. And from what I can see in it, it has the spirit that only masterpieces can generate.

Of course this work can be analysed in more academic and orthodox terms. And so one must point out the undoubtable weight of the piranesian monumentality of the stairs, and the way the tension of its roof references a similar tension a thousand miles away in the Dulles airport, Chicago, designed by Eero Saarinen, where a sheet of concrete is suspended on strained pillars in an extremely familiar way to this stadium. And where the geometry of the catenary and the inclination of the supports help the natural stability of the whole structure. As would be done with a canopy.

Reference should also be made to a closer, only slightly older construction of two renowned Portuguese architects, Álvaro Siza and Eduardo Souto de Moura, who, in the Lisbon Pavilion, constructed in 1998, suspended a similar sheet of concrete on pillars, creating a shadowed square. But where the effort to support the sheet was hidden between static, serene piers, in an almost Italian way...

But, is it important to know who created the concrete crustacean which is the Municipal Stadium of Braga? Perhaps not.

We said that we are standing before a masterpiece. However, we cannot forget that, as a typology, masterpieces require a certain innocence from their creators. Therefore, when one is made, the very concept of creatorship is overwhelmed by the construction which in some way swallows its creator. In this sense, the writer Flaubert lamented that the vulgar maid Madame Bovary had achieved greater immortality than himself. How was it possible that a fictitious character could be assured life and fame throughout time? Will something similar happen with the Municipal Stadium of Braga? What does its author think about it? What does Souto de Moura think?

I

From the very beginning, Eduardo Souto de Moura has enjoyed an unusual amount of attention from specialists. Architectural publications quickly took notice of Álvaro Siza's young collaborator who had already constructed a detached house from ruin in Gerês and the up-and-coming market in the city of Braga at the start of the 80s; and who showed a way of creating architecture without the same predisposition towards sculpturing as his master, but with a sensitivity to the materials and their memory that was uncommon in the Portuguese scene at that time.

As years have gone by, and as more constructions have been built an[d] been added to his professional repertoire, Souto de Moura has become an extremely popular architect even among those who don't specialise in the field. Although arriving there took more than two decades, the fact that he has designed the residence of the most famous footballer in the world attests to the unusual resonance that his work has, even in his own country. However, and distressingly for Souto de Moura, that popularity is based on a permanent misunderstanding. And it is from there precisely that some of the discomfort with which he develops his work derives. A misunderstanding due to which his followers have populated Portugal with elemental boxes of the purest "Souto de Moura style"–which he refers to, without a hint of irony, with the term "microwaves"–and which have made his work susceptible to being under permanent formal scrutiny as these followers search for new material to imitate.

Perhaps the world of easy acquisition and distribution of images in which we have been immersed contributes to this. But the truth is that the difficulty of carrying out a profound reading into Souto de Moura's architecture through these photographs has impeded the true understanding of his works, which may seem easy to imitate, but only if one doesn't pay enough attention to their more complex and more subt[le] details. T.S. Eliot said the following regarding the relationship between a master, his disciples, and imitation:

> A true disciple is impressed by what his master has to say, an[d] *consequently* by his way of saying it; an imitator–I might say, a borrower– is impressed chiefly by the way the master said it. [If] he manages to mimic his master well enough, he may suceed even is disguising from himself the fact that he has nothing to say.[1]

1.
Eliot, T. S., *To Criticize the Critic and Other Writings*, University of Nebraska Press, Lincoln, 1992, p. 54

These problems, both that of being imitated in shallow way, and being considered a master, have troubled Souto de Moura for different reason[s].

On the other hand, "Souto de Moura style" is a paradox within itself. It is not easy to divide such a diverse catalogue into the conceptual labels with which attempts have been made to classify it. Labelled as a localist by Kenneth Frampton, promoter of the memorable phrase "critical regionalism", however this concept hardly helps to understand the Portuguese phenomenon in all his complexity, and even less, to encompass a work which is much more than an ambiguous "laconic tradition" linked to modernity. In addition, the fact that the context in which Souto de Moura, Álvaro Siza and Fernando Távora work has been named "Porto School" by other people is perhaps what has created this term. The so-called "Porto School", in fact, has left its members in a territory in which none seems to feel comfortable.

However, the above does not mean that criticism of Souto de Moura's work has been unproductive or lacking in insight. Nevertheless, the main avenues of analysis have always highlighted all kinds of continuities: with the city of Porto, and with Siza and Távora, or analysed the influence of Mies Van der Rohe, de Rossi, popular architecture, and the work of his most contemporary colleagues on his works. In the last instance, the approaches of Antonio Esposito and Giovanni Leoni, Nuno Grande, and most recently in purely visual terms, of Juan Antonio Cortés, have been even closer and far-reaching because they have found a way of unravelling the work of a figure who refuses to exercise the uncertain role of being a master, to speak about style, and even to be understood from a type of reductionist elementism.

In a way, Souto de Moura has remained resistant to every attempt to unify his work. None of the critics attempts seem to have been able to expose a clear storyline within his body of work. Not even when they have tried to establish fragile periods, groups or thematic familiarities, has the result seemed fully satisfactory. The leaps between his works are so great, not only at design level but also in terms of solutions and internal logic, that the label "heteronymy" falls short. Nonetheless, it has become apparent that every attempt to unify his work is futile. And this is because in the case of Souto de Moura, it is really difficult to penetrate his conceptual shield which, in any case, does not seem to be voluntary nor made by himself. Neither is it perhaps based on some unfading, theoretical assumptions, rather it is the direct result of the way each project is forged and its concrete circumstances. Souto de Moura himself seems to be trying to figure out his true way of working and his own role in architecture. He rummages around his own creations as an architect, just as the critics have tried to, except using the project itself and the act of design as a basis. In other words, one can sense a supplementary effort in Souto de Moura; an introspection into what architecture is and what its relative position is in the face of these brilliant, beautiful, unattainable objects around which its activity orbits. And by doing so, he undoubtedly distances himself from Siza, for whom this same question is futile, because he does not see architecture as a phenomenon outside of itself. Or for Távora, for whom this question about architecture is answered in each of his works in terms of pure continuity; as any cultural phenomenon does...

Moura

III

Twenty years separate Eduardo Souto de Moura and Álvaro Siza. Likewise, thirty years separate him from Fernando Távora. The generational difference between them, their own declarations of admiration and familiarity, plus their evident reciprocal intellectual debts, should suffice in order to understand why any attempt to simplify this network by calling it a "school" is difficult to work with. Justifying just one of the works of these architects by its relationship to the others might uncover a deep system of communicating vessels, however, surely, it is something more speculative than real. The origin of these mutual influences is based on something more than mere intentions or respect; it derives from a centre which is outside the scope of conventional criticism because it touches upon areas of psychology, or at least, pure hermeneutics.

Yet, the way in which these three very different architects have hybridized their work occurs in a very strange way in modern architecture, since it doesn't just happen through downward chain, rather in a reciprocal and alternative way, rich and unpredictable, leaping through ages, and moments throughout the years, with periods of overlap, closeness, or distance in the interests of each one of them. Álvaro Siza himself put his finger on it when he recognised his debt not only to Távora but also, in a bidirectional sense, to Souto de Moura:

> I make no bones in admitting the influence was reciprocal, something I've perhaps never fully explored.[2]

That is why when Fernando Távora speaks about the link he has with Siza and Eduardo Souto de Moura in terms of a common "house", he doesn't just do so in a literal sense, referring to the building where they all share space, rather he refers to the way the "house" took shape. Maybe that's why Távora himself began to refer to this shared space and network of connections as a "cathedral of architecture", highlighting that what draws them together is reminiscent of a climate which is similar to, or rather, which existed between medieval architects and the great spiritual spaces of the Gothic era.[3] Among them there is indeed an intellectual infiltration, which transcends a mere transference of ideas, forms and stylistic features. And that's why it has outgrown its participants and forces us to ask a bigger question, which is difficult to answer: What is the channel through which this expertise is transmitted? What is the connection, the climate, that subsumes that of mere physical proximity so that the influence is given as a true fact?

Some time ago Giorgio Grassi said, with regards to mastery, that there are two different types: that of the masters that encourage us, that support us in moments of hardship, that cheer us on, and accompany us, in a nutshell the "tutelary" masters. And then there are the others,

2. Esposito, Antonio and Leoni, Giovanni, *Eduardo Souto de Moura*. Phaidon, London, 2013. p. 9

3. Esposito, Antonio and Leoni, Giovanni, *op. cit.* p. 14

those who set the standard for what the profession means, those that leave us in solitude and demand solitude from us, those who torture us with their demands and prevent us from falling into a complacency that easy work would bring.[4] Grassi forgot to say that mastery generates a moral yearning that has an important covert clause, which is essential not to ignore in the case of Souto de Moura: unfortunately, being the said child of a master, and even his mere proximity to one, means he has received an inheritance that can leave one buried underneath the burden of paralysis and infidelity. Actually, how has Souto de Moura circumvented the the responsibility of that close mastery of Távora and Siza? Where can a dignified disciple to continue that chain be found? And what does the contemporary update of the same word "mastery" imply in the case of Souto de Moura, in a profession and at a time where architecture remains very far from all the professional relationships that a word such as "mastery" implies, and where the word itself seems to have been understood as a licence without limits to perpetrate any piece of architecture? Souto de Moura gives a clearly defined answer when he places value on anonymity as a legitimate way of exercising his profession.[5] And at the same time he situates himself, with regards to Siza and Távora, free from the suffocating pressure of their expertise. (Until he mysteriously produces a masterpiece, of course.)

In fact, the case of these three architects would be an optimum place to understand, at the present day, what the real virality of knowledge of this discipline implies, before understanding the architecture of Porto or their individual works. And, although the declarations of those involved about the intimate operation of that chain usually lack importance, nobody has said it more and more clearly than Souto de Moura himself:

> There isn't a direct exchange of architectural influences but that's no quite true in my case. I feel I have received direct influences, perhaps not direct borrowings, but if, for instance, I have to refubrish an old building, it's difficult for me not to think of Távora. If I have to design a window I think almost automatically of the Ofir House. It's obviously not a question of vocabulary or style, rather of method. I don't think about the window in itself but I think of its proportions, the way it opens in a wall. The same thing happens with Siza. Not everything can be a right angle, and whenever I've designed a narrow house on a road where it was impossible to keep tha walls straight, though I've never drawn curved lines I think of Siza. I assess their works one by one, I don't let myself get carried away by their tone. I consider them a subconscious Neufert, something that emerges in certain situations.[6]

4. Grassi, Giorgio, *Architecture Dead Language*, Electa/Rizzoli, Milan/New York, 1988.

5. "As far as I'm concerned, it is evident that my ambition is to be anonymous. Because when one remains encoded, one stays anonymous" in Grande, Nuno, "A conversation with Eduardo Souto de Moura", *El Croquis* nº 146, *Souto de Moura, 2005-2009, Theaters of the world*, El croquis editorial, El Escorial, 2009. p. 23

6. Esposito, Antonio and Leoni, Giovanni, *op. cit.* p. 14

On the other hand, and if it is difficult to speak about the works of Eduardo Souto de Moura according to his relationship with those tutelary masters, neither is it reassuring to do so within the network of influences marked by the purely physical context of Portugal. Moving forward with some ideas, it can be said that his works themselves give reason to believe that there are many Souto de Mouras in the architect Eduardo Souto de Moura. Or at least, there has been an attempt to blur his protagonism: a willingness for anonymity and to avoid any hint of mastery, which has also been achieved due to his conviction that there are other ways of understanding the work of an architect aside from his genius. Perhaps that is why Souto de Moura has highlighted the importance of second-generation architects, for example, when he declared his admiration for Jorge Segurado, or for Alberto Pessoa, Ruy d'Athouguia and Pedro Cid, designers of the Calouste Gulbenkian Museum and headquarters in Lisbon, among others.[7]

7. Morales, José, "Domesticating architecture. A conversation with Eduardo Souto de Moura", *El croquis nº 176, Eduardo Souto de Moura 2009-2014*, El croquis Editorial, El Escorial, 2014. pp. 6ff.

Putting the focus on this second generation means that one must stop considering the history of Portuguese architecture as a mere succession of great architects, start seeing it as a great collection of part of a larger set of European and Western architecture. The nebula of constructions works and architects which lie outside of historical the focus of history is the one that which has built the panorama through which the survival of the cities has occurred and which has also sustains the climate and the atmosphere in which Siza and Távora also create their works. It's a complex ecosystem which is not easy to simplify under any label, such as "school".

IV

Three groups of corners. Of these, the Braga Market is the symbol of the first group. But, which Braga Market? The one built by young Souto de Moura in 1977? Or the one that was demolished by the other, mature, skeptical Souto de Moura twenty years later? In reality, the attitudes and changes that have occurred between these two versions of the same architect do not matter, neither do their traumas nor their joys, because the walls have stayed upright in the face of any quarrelling or settling of scores. The corners have defended themselves from the demolition, although this was not so with the roof which has been removed and turned into a courtyard and a garden. The corners have been maintained and are lengthened by the placement of downpipes which pin the design to the ground. These heavy walls extend, and the way they have been constructed is far from abstract due to their strong materiality. Although at the beginning, there is one wall that dares to float (just like in the Art Gallery in Praça de Lisboa or inside the Casa das Artes in Porto).

Corners from this group, which are more edges than corners, form a part of many of the walls of the houses built in the first decade of Souto de Moura's career, such as the houses in Negovilde, the courtyard houses de of Matosinhos (1993-1999) and the Casa das Artes in Porto (1981-1991). All of them explore a language of levels which overgrow and glide from a fictitious closed structure. In all of these cases, the walls are massive and in many cases they contribute to the stability of the terrain because they support the land on the other side. When the wall comes to an end, the corners are a sign of construction, and they have been opened up to show their insides. Although not in a harsh manner, unlike in some of Rem Koolhaas' constructions. Instead, it is done with the care of somebody who wants to show the how constructive these layers which form the walls can be. Souto de Moura says the following about these corners and why they show their overlapping levels:

> A twenty-centimeter-thick stone wall no longer responds to the different behaviour of materials on the outside, on the inside, on the skin and in the structure, and then there is the damn thermal brdge to be resolved, obliging us to lie, to go on changing.[8]

In contrast to the corners of a wall constructed by Mies, those by Souto de Moura don't pretend to be of a single width, instead they accept their own complexity. And it's impossible to leave to one side the ways with which Mies and Souto de Moura address the finishing of these edges. The former, with a massive piece of the same material, which is reminiscent of the onyx walls of the Barcelona pavilion, and the latter by exfoliating the wall's layers. The complex primitivism of leaving the real widths of these edges for all to see is halfway between delicate and the way in which one would expect popular, anonymous architecture to address this wall specialisation. And in a certain sense it makes one of the walls appear to have predated the other. In fact, could it be possible that Souto de Moura is a predecessor of Mies Van der Rohe? Sometimes poetry is more real than history: Mies' brick house undoubtedly copies Eduardo Souto de Moura and represents an advancement in his work, the way in which his walls have freed themselves from the need to contain land. And if this is so plausible, it is because in some secret way the work of Souto de Moura has altered the way we look at the works of Mies Van der Rohe himself. From Souto de Moura we can sense a much more impure and complex facet of the German architect, and this goes beyond what Rowe detected in that corner of the Seagram building which covered the structure with bronze profiles.

This game of diluting and temporality is one of the central problems when it comes to interpreting the work of Souto de Moura. And it seems

8.
Souto de Moura, Eduardo, "Nexus", in Esposito, Antonio y Leoni, Giovanni, *op. cit.* p. 374

Mercado de Carandá.
Braga, Portugal.
1980–2001

to start precisely from a point where what is modern is either about to be defined, or has been completely surpassed, or from a point where modernity is being discussed, be it because of primitivism or due to postmodernity.

The second group of corners can be found in the Rua do Teatro building. An apartment building has been directed with all of its being to face the street. It does this because of the arrangement of the structures of varying different sizes. The steel frame which covers the façade is elegant and sophisticated, with steel profiles of equal dimensions, despite which are able to hide the real constructive thickness of the floors, walls, and roof covering. This is not a minor detail with which to understand the types of constructive strategy that Souto de Moura likes to employ. The fact is that there is no simple way to make it seem like a roof has the same thickness as the floor of an intermediate level, at least in the technological and cultural context of construction in Portugal. Because, usually at this point the insulation and the watertightness of the building should be addressed, and it's obvious they don't occupy the same space.

In addition, the façade's steel frame is given priority through the direction of the placement of its profile: one direction, with the main elevation facing the street. The same detail on each one of the joints between the horizontal and vertical profiles shows a narrative of "fronts and sides" and a constructive order, which highlights the prominence of each edge.

The profiles in H, shadow profiles, shoot off in one direction, we could say, and this gesture applies to the entire the work. So much so that anyone who takes the necessary time to observe the floors will see that even the interior partitions themselves, despite their apparent looseness and freedom, have been redirected and corrected at the last moment so that they arrive at this steel frame without modifying its layout. Meanwhile, the sides of these boxes become pure secondary façades, covered in slate with without any gaps being opened inside them.

These structures, careful with their scale in relation to the rest of the neighbourhood, remain pure, without breaks or strident gestures in their outer walls. They have that American air possessed by the buildings designed by SOM in the sixties. Their language can be understood within the logic of a canonic modernity in relation to the structure. However, inside, they follow a somewhat anomalous compositional law, which in no way appears coherent with this steel grid that forms cornered boxes on the outside. Souto de Moura is conscious of the strangeness of this situation, in which it seems as if the family of shapes from his first walled houses has been covered by a cubed carcass:

Casa das Artes.
Porto, Portugal. 1980

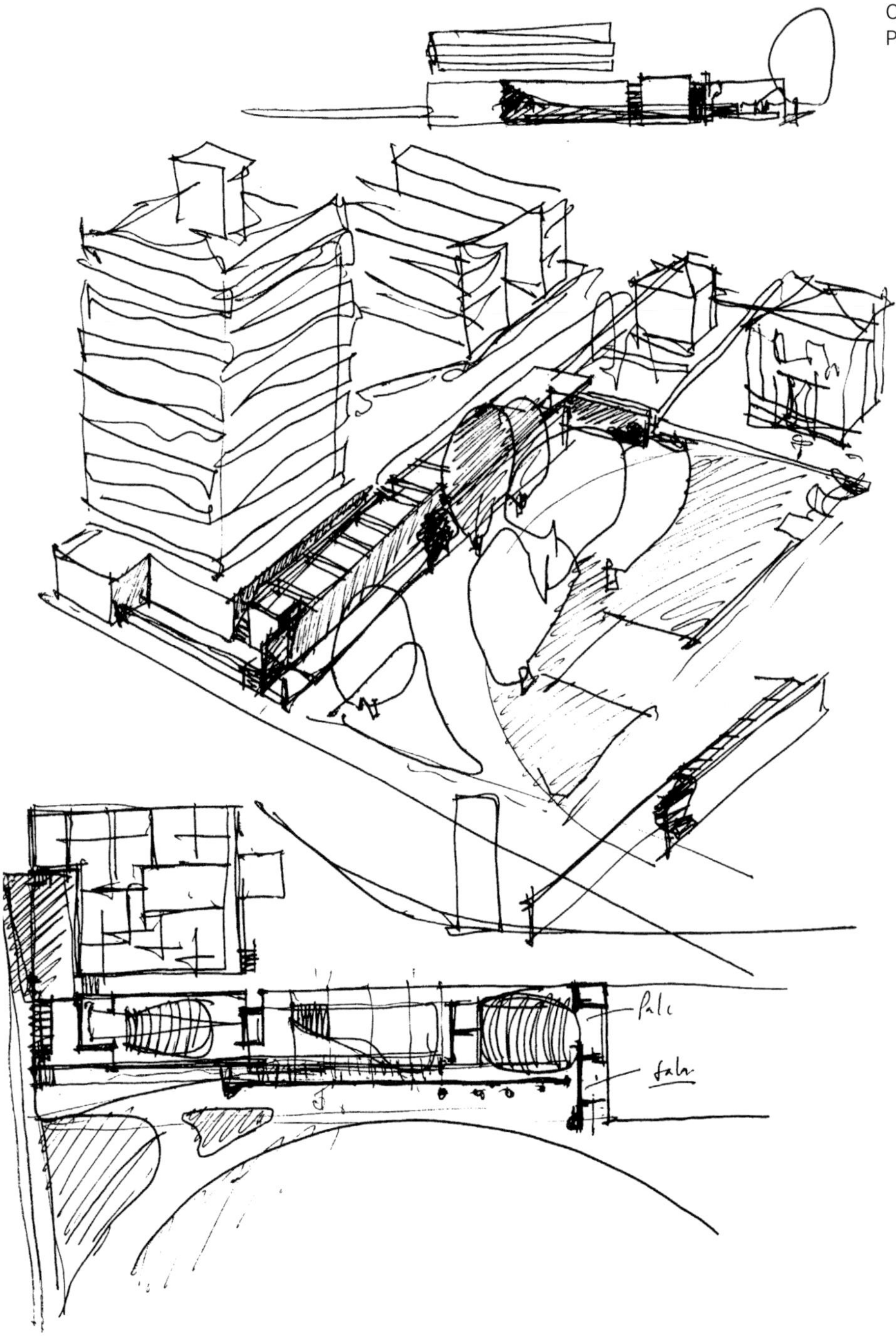

> In designing the interiors in detail, I followed a method very close to what is called "neo-plasticism" (...) This "neo-plastic" atmosphere of the apartments was not the result of my personal acceptance of the poetics of neo-plasticism: I simply use the methods of neo-plasticism architects conciously to subdivide and recompose the spaces to suit the different situations that came up.[9]

9. Souto de Moura, Eduardo, "High-Rise Blocks", in Esposito, Antonio and Leoni, Giovanni, *op. cit.* p. 215

To understand the difficulty of making any connection between the Rua do Teatro building and neoplasticism, which, nevertheless, might have been upheld in the cases of the walls from the first group of corners, it may be convenient to remember that the main goal of old neoplasticist poetry was focused on the dissolution of the box as a compositional artifice. The architecture of Frank Lloyd Wright, from the Robie, Usonian and Prairie Houses, and all the architecture of Mies van der Rohe, were founded on the simplicity of a discovery that placed the focus on the corners of architecture.

The box was free from its bearing ties, and the levels of its faces were no more than abstract objects. One only has to remember the Schröder house in Ulbrecht by Gerrit Rietveld, for example, to understand how the deployment of the box within the space suggested an attempt to blur all possible limitations, including the difference between the interior and the exterior. From that point the preeminence of a discussion based on all dialects of main and secondary façades became, apparently, of secondary importance. And the discussion of the material tilted towards the abstract, filling the walls with flat, weightless colours.

However, and if we have already seen the preference for substance in the neoplastic walls of Souto de Moura, in this work, the rationale that there is decomposition in the levels is already very weakened. So much so that there is not even enough musculature to undo the corners of those well-formed boxes. The edges here are not free from the responsibility of sustaining the weight of the work, but rather the total opposite occurs: they are highlighted with steel lines. This blatant contradiction between a box and its neoplastic interior would not leave any modern spirit alone. So what kind of conceptual game allows a building to freely indulge in different compositional systems without destroying its coherence? It only occurs to me to answer that it is a kind of logic protected under a certain postmodern disbelief. Or under the spirit of an authentic *bricoleur*...

To this issue, where only the material in its detail tries to extend, we could add cases such as that of the office tower in Burgo. In the corners of that building, the strips of the façade are separated or overlapped in order to show an alternative rhythm of stacking, reminiscent both of

Office building on the Boavista-Burgo avenue. Porto, Portugal. 1991

the way in which wooden trunks are accumulated in kilns and of some children's games played with wooden pieces. But at the same time, there the exercises of construction and scale are once again subtle. By observing the corners, it is once again possible to determine which façade demands the most attention, but this is only noticeable via a slight suggestion, offered by showing the edge of the material, which is lighter and thinner than one would usually expect from granite, but that still sticks out and extends like weightless levels in each piece: a corner like a neoplastic miniature on a 2:1 scale.

The third group of corners concerns the breaking of the structure at its edges. At those points, the box is emptied or intersected with structures that are placed at the edges, as in the Casa do Cinema (Cinema House) of Manoel de Oliveira. In any case, the emptiness at those points disrupts the sense of weight that every large, opaque box has, turning volume into a game which is close to something sculptural, but where everything gets lightened and becomes more ethereal and airy.

The systematisation of that language of absent corners is remarkable in the Paula Rego Museum. In the halls, by opening up those points, the potential system of corridors which every museum would want in order to help with expository logic is unravelled. Each room opens to the outside, or to other rooms, at its broken corners. However, it is done by reducing the scale precisely at the transition points. The "breaks" are always characterised by either a door or a window, steps or an alcove – a singular point. The loss of a recognisable language, and his anonymity represents a unsettling qualitative leap in Souto de Moura's work. In these corners, there is no longer a recognisable Souto de Moura, rather other types of influences appear. And opportunities.

This same issue of corners that bite into the structure does not have to be exclusively applied to vertical edges and levels. This emptying can also be done with the floor plan, as occurs in the Museum of Contemporary Art in Bragança, where contact with the floor becomes a place to play with the weight of the building itself.

The combination of these three types of corners may be enough to indicate how much we are talking about an architecture that must be addressed, and understood in terms of pure language and its syntax. In the architecture of Souto de Moura, the fact that the character of architecture is understood as an ordered set of shapes. capable of constructing a meaning, can also be understood by the means of the approach offered by the references used.[10]

o.
ı the Paula Rego
useum, for example,
ıe influence of Rossi, of
ıeetings with Siza or on
ıe local architect Raul
ino, are made clear
nd make the work an
malgamation of *objets*
ouvés.

V

Souto de Moura is an exemplary collagist, an exceptional collector of architectural objects that are wisely arranged in his works. However, the edges of these objects are carefully rehabilitated in their second use in order to erase their border. Each object, each encounter, and each loan has been carefully polished. There are no lumps of glue or rough welds as happened in the early three dimensional collages of Picasso and Schwitters. The world of *objets trouvés* according to Souto de Moura is a world without dust or dirtiness. That is his biggest interpretive problem. His works are collages that occur with no visible conflict. They are camouflaged by elementarism. Except in the place where no piece of collage is able to hide: the corners.

What is the Viana do Castelo pavilion without the facilities shaped as if they were crowned by the hats made of bay leaves that old Olympians used to wear? Or without keeping in mind the inevitable reference to the Pompidou museum? What is the Braga stadium without a great Greek theatre? What are the rehabilitations of Santa María do Bouro and the Porto subway, but works without an author, infrastructure, where the *bricoleur* has managed to camouflage himself in anonymity, where the architect is hidden?...

Collage is systematically used by Souto de Moura but if it is so difficult to detect it is because, contrary to what one might expect, an enormous effort has been made to hide the conflicts and the edges. To mitigate the contradictions until even the author himself disappears.

In this regard, little critical attention has been paid to a text which, despite its short length, is significant in helping to understand Souto de Moura's way of doing things: "Nexus", is composed of fragments of a purest Benjamin style, and where his interest in a method close to cinematographic montage is evident:

> I rewrite it like a collage: they are other people's words, made my own. I don't even know the names of some of them. It is like a conditioned reflex, a bit of vertigo on paper.[11]

The important thing about collage according to Souto de Moura is that, with it, some of the needs and traumas of modernity disappear. With it, it is possible to say new things with used things. With it, the creator is not obliged to be under the weight and the curse of making something from scratch, rather to bring existing pieces together better. Collage works for Souto de Moura because it allows him to fill the monstrous gap between architecture and life. Precisely between the world of the building and the world of its inhabitants, is a territory that has been overlooked, but that Souto de Moura is interested in, because within it he senses the modern and postmodern trauma in which contemporary architecture can be found. This intermediate territory is a fertile space for misunderstanding,

11. Souto de Moura, Eduardo, "Nexus", in Esposito, Antonio y Leoni, Giovanni, *op. cit.* p. 373

but also for errors and crossroads. It is the space between what was planned in the design and what really happens to architecture once it is inhabited.

The twentieth century allowed us to see collage as a way of breaking free from academia and specialization. Bricolage doesn't require theories, or sophisticated prior knowledge. Today we know that collage is the most accurate means to describe the way in which inhabitants take ownership of architecture. For Souto de Moura, collage means the full and liberating awareness of how little an architect knows, of how little he controls the shape and even the final result. Souto de Moura has discovered for us that architecture receives its meaning from life and not from its author. That awareness may be the central component of his mastery.

Souto de Mou

FUMADORES
SMOKERS
FUMEURS

Block in Senhora da Luz: the Windows and the Sea

panoramah!®

Location:
Porto, Portugal

Client:
LPSM, Empreendimento Sra. da Luz

Project:
2009–2014

Completion:
2016

Architecture:
Souto Moura Arquitectos Lda

Author:
Eduardo Souto de Moura

Collaborators:
André Campos
Luis Peixoto
José Carlos Mariano
Ana Patrícia Sobral
Maria Otília Aires Pereira
Susana Oliveira Marques
Rute Peixoto

Structural Engineering:
Rui Furtado
Carlos Quinaz
AFAconsult

Electrical Engineering:
Maria da Luz
AFAconsult

Mechanical Engineering:
Marco Carvalho
AFAconsult

Contractor:
Matriz Sociedade de Construções Lda

Text:
Carlos Machado e Moura

Photographs:
Luís Ferreira Alves

This rigorous and contained building at the seafront of Porto–a monochrome block, with three apartments, accessible by a narrow alley, a communal roof terrace, a commercial space on the ground floor and an underground car park–is a far more complex and singular work than it might seem at first sight.

The process of conception and construction lasted long, not without surprises, and was marked by a great self-criticism, since Eduardo Souto de Moura made a building for himself, being at the same time client and real estate developer. In the constant search for a method and an architectural language, the relation between the house and the ocean reveals the importance of the window.

1.

A contemporary building with generous views of the Atlantic was the first intention. It occupies two rectangular plots between Rua de São Bartolomeu and the elevated seafront (Rua Coronel Raul Peres), replacing the derelict buildings that once housed the public bathrooms for the beach. The volume was already determined by the adjacent building and the height limited by the 45° rule, which imposed four storeys, one of which set back on the east façade.

However, in that listed area of Foz do Douro surrounding Rua da Senhora da Luz, the Heritage Protection Authority prescribed the recreation of old façades and stone masonry, despite the contemporary architectures already present. Studies of volume and façade succeeded, and the large glazed windows were progressively overlaid with *brise-soleils*. A modern grid of classical composition and a very strong tectonic structure became the solution. In a concrete reinterpretation of the traditional stone post and lintel structure of the buildings along the Douro River front, Souto de Moura found a principle of composition that served both the façades of the building.

Being a housing programme, sun control and privacy to the interiors was required, controlling the openings of the bedrooms and creating shelter and comfort for the living rooms facing the immensity of the sea. The façades were recessed about 60 cm, evoking the stone balconies of Portuguese vernacular architecture. In the elevation of the rooms, this solution allowed to fit the wardrobes, creating enclosed elements in the concrete frame and giving the façade a new thickness.

In the opposite side, facing the sea, vertical concrete elements –which became loadbearing– introduced the desired protection, creating a sense of distance. The depth of the septa cuts the sea vertically from a side view, while allowing its plenitude to be revealed in a frontal view, perfectly framed. To emphasize this effect, the septa have a trapezoidal horizontal section, reducing their expression on the inner side, approaching that of the window frames, and reaching the same thickness of the slabs on the outer face. This game is altered in the rear façade, where the variations of thickness occur in vertical section, on the tops of the slabs. The metal railing, placed on the outside, offers each room a small balcony, while on the west façade, facing the sea, it is deliberately set back, leaving the concrete grid untouched and assuming the house ends by the glass pane. These elements thus become a protection for the sun and the sea, not an extension of the house. It is this small gesture that replaces the building's domestic dimension by giving it a different, more urban and abstract scale, before the sea.

2.

Once the proportions of the concrete grid determined the expression of the building, the work on a second layer arises: the window frames. The location in an historical area advised the use of wood (with 12 cm thick frames), which would result in an image close to a certain Swiss architecture or to some works by Louis Kahn. However, the choice of reinforced concrete and the modern language of the structure led Souto de Moura to prefer aluminium painted RAL 9006 for the seaside lacquage durability. The building thus remained without any concessions in terms of materials, only a tectonic allusion to vernacular architecture.

As for the windows, with the vertical frames hidden by the concrete septa, all the design focused on the threshold, the only visible element, desirably with the least possible expression. The minimalist window thus became natural among the range of options, and the sliding system offered indubitably the greatest flexibility behind the concrete grid.

On the western façade, the main challenges were the strong pressure of the wind and the constant sound of the often-turbulent sea. **panoramah!®** featured a reinforced frame and a triple glass solution with great inertia. To its excellent acoustic insulation – obtained by laminated glass with acoustic pvb – is combined efficient solar control performance and the perfectly transparent low-iron glass, which sets the ideal contemplation of the sea. By slightly sliding the sash, the sound of the waves returns, adding the acoustic perception to the visual panorama.

The solution was adapted to the effective needs, with triple glass in the west elevation facing the sea (series **ah!54**) and double glass in the north and east elevations with kitchens and bedrooms (series **ah!38**). Other details and small customizations were also developed specifically for this work: a cremone bolt designed by Souto de Moura, shotbolts on the central mullions and a different corner assembly of the profiles.

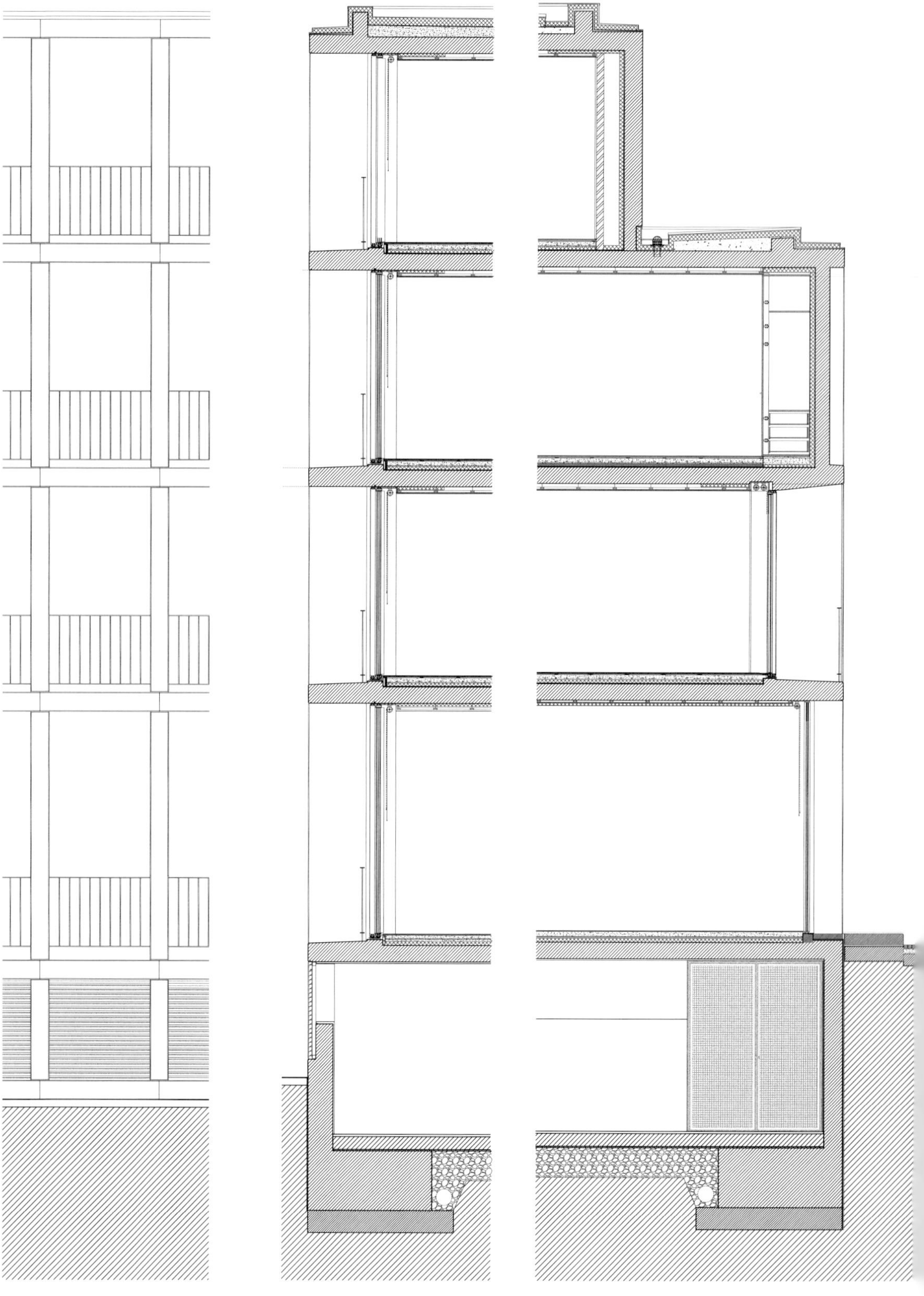

Elevation
Section

3.

Several unforeseen events marked the progress of this work. A water line under the old bathrooms building (once used for the baths) made difficult the realization and waterproofing of the garage. A dispute with a neighbour during the construction forced a change in the design and the introduction of a recess in the middle of the north façade, introducing a new small balcony in the kitchens. These and other unexpected events moulded and transformed the pure shape of the first models, adapting to the various conditionings dictated by the surroundings and giving the volume an unexpected plastic expression.

If the inexorable logic of the two main façades seems to determine this building, the perspective point of view we always have from it, due to the narrow width of the streets, shows us that its beauty emerges not only from its rigor but also from the ability to accept contradiction and provide scale and sense to a difficult part of the city. Between the new blocks and the small houses of Senhora da Luz, amongst ramps, tunnels, stairs and alleys, in a viaduct-like elevated seafront that has not yet re-found its naturalness as street, this building has its *raison d'être* on the windows and the sea.

qbo
light4you

qboiluminacion.com

Capri Lounge + Reverse Occasional

DEKTON®
designed by COSENTINO
Redefining Surfaces.
Redefining Limits.
Dekton Ultracompact breaks down architectural boundaries and reimagines spaces to become infinite.
We have redefined concepts to create a revolutionary and versatile material with a unique design, format and resistance.

Inspiring people through
innovative spaces

Inspirar la vida de las personas
a través de espacios innovadores

COSENTINO®

cosentino.com / silestone.com / dekton.com

GANDIABLASCO SHOWROOMS

SOLANAS

DANIEL GERMANI

gandiablasco.com

Porto: T. +351 22 618 13 55 gbporto@gandiablasco.com

Lisboa: T. +351 21 396 23 38 gblisboa@gandiablasco.com

CHIC STAYS
COMPORTA BLISS
CHATEAU LIFE
BIG BOOK OF THE HAMPTONS

Custom Integrated Technology

LLEDO

lledogrupo.com
Cid Campeador, 14. 28935 Móstoles. Madrid
T. +34 916 656 180

Pizarras Universal

Pizarras Universal is situated in Spain, in the northern zone of Galicia in Pastoriza, Lugo. It is a world leader in the extraction and fabrication of FILITA in green, grey, and black varieties. The special characteristics of the different varieties allow for a wide range of possibilities to which the chance of using different sizes and thicknesses must be added. These can be used in roofs, and also in ventilated façades, pavements and furniture.

Limited Edition

Pizarras Universal

universalpizarras@outlook.es

T. +34 982 349 329

Traducciones en español

Editorial

Dedicar un número de *Archives* a Eduardo Souto de Moura parece un reto complejo: su obra es suficientemente conocida y no suele esconder aquellos temas que aborda o le interesan. Uno tiene la sensación de que conoce lo que se pueda escribir sobre ese conjunto que forma el arquitecto y su obra, pero lo cierto es que no está todo escrito y ni tan siquiera intuido. También parece que su obra está fotografiada abundantemente. Sin embargo, *Archives* tiene que mostrar esa mirada distinta de las imágenes de Juan Rodríguez, que, en el caso de Eduardo Souto, no es una mirada centrada en un tiempo corto, sino en uno dilatado de quien ya ha fotografiado buena parte de sus obras y le ha acompañado en sus viajes. El texto crece en este número añadiendo la mirada certera de Santiago de Molina, buscando la lectura que facilita el formato elegido para *Archives*.

Los dibujos rápidos y certeros de Eduardo tienen siempre que acompañar la explicación de su obra, esos dibujos que realiza mientras resume cada una de las obras con la mayor de las precisiones. Son dibujos de escasos minutos que parecen sintetizar muchos años de trabajo y a los que se suman las imágenes de aquellas obras anónimas que mira atentamente.

Pedro Cabrita Reis ha sido el artista que eligió para acompañarle. En esa selección no solo ayudan una relación personal intensa y muchos trabajos en común: también el complemento de la mirada de Eduardo hacía Pedro y viceversa deberían ayudar a completar esa mirada amplia de Souto.

Pedro Cabrita también aparece en la colección de 24 imágenes sin texto: es una de las veinticuatro personas que configuran lo que llama sus «*santinhos*», veinticuatro personas que configuran un universo que le interesa. Ante el esfuerzo de explicar los aspectos de cada uno de ellos que le han llegado a influir, prefiere que aparezca simplemente un retrato que resuma todo aquello que podamos imaginar que ha podido extraer de su trabajo o de sus postulados.

La pasión y la obstinación

Carlos Quintáns

La obra de Eduardo Souto de Moura es muy conocida. Para muchos, su arquitectura es aparentemente reconocible y algunos piensan que, además, es previsible. Sin embargo, la sensación de no encontrar los límites de su trabajo anida en quien se fija en el estadio de Braga, en el museo Paula Rego o, recientemente, en Barrocal, por poner algunos ejemplos. Su arquitectura es un constante avanzar y revisar que se puntea con momentos excepcionales.

La suya es una forma de hacer que le lleva a remirar y reformular su trabajo a la vez que que hace lo mismo con el de aquellos que admira. Le gusta explicar como Thomas Bernhard siempre escribe el mismo libro, como se detiene en el detalle con minuciosidad obsesiva, avanza un paso y retrocede para volver sobre lo mismo. Podríamos considerar que estamos ante alguien que formula unos procedimientos de trabajo de los que salen proyectos que, si bien pueden considerarse aislados, debemos mirar en conjunto. Yo me atrevería a proponer una mirada en su totalidad para presentarla como hizo Herberto Helder cuando decidió reunir su poesía completa y la rehízo toda en un poema único: *Ou o poema contínuo*.

Esta mirada hacia las constantes y las variantes en la obra de Eduardo pueden acercarlo al jazz, del que tanto disfruta y en el que le gusta verse acompañado por Miles Davis o por Ahmad Jamal. Resulta curioso que las primeras descripciones de Ahmad hablan de su uso consciente de los espacios y de los silencios para subrayar los tránsitos entre la relajación y la tensión, caracterizado por una gran economía de medios y líneas melódica y armónicamente inventivas.

Casualidades o no, lo cierto es que Eduardo gusta de acompañarse de la búsqueda en otras disciplinas, especialmente en la literatura y en la música, sin olvidar el cine, la pintura ni, obviamente, la escultura, búsqueda en la que prima la vuelta hacia lo conocido frente al intento de capturar la novedad. ¿Novedad? Me lo imagino comentando, argumentando con una pregunta la explicación de quien cree que tan solo podemos reelaborar y no inventar.

La búsqueda de procedimientos de trabajo aparece continuamente en sus conversaciones: Rainer Maria Rilke, Enrique Vila-Matas o Mario Vargas Llosa le interesan por ello más que por su obra. Y en esa búsqueda también llega a la arquitectura al hablar de Aldo Rossi y su *Autobiografía científica* o la *Arquitectura de la ciudad*. Su primer contacto con Rossi en Santiago de Compostela, al igual que la relación con sus libros, son citas permanentes en sus entrevistas. El libro *Architektur* (1989) de Donald Judd también es otra constante.

Son pocos los cambios en su selección de referentes. Lector incansable y obsesivo, comprador de libros y viajero permanente.

Su despacho dentro del estudio contiene las publicaciones que usa: algunos libros de Mies (su colección de distintas ediciones de publicaciones de Mies es muy grande y no está aquí toda), el *Inquérito*, algunos otros libros de arquitectura popular portuguesa y el orgullo de que presidan el espacio todos los números de *Tectónica* al lado de algunos de otra revista.

Eduardo escribe poco y cuando lo hace ocupa una buena parte de su texto con alguna referencia literaria, con la humildad de quien reconoce inalcanzable la perfección que otros logran. Se siente cómodo hablando mientras dibuja muy rápido, con trazo vigoroso, esos dibujos que aparecen en sus libros y que deben entenderse como el acompañamiento de la palabra. También se siente cómodo en las entrevistas, aunque, como acostumbra a contestar, «Não tenho nada novo para lhe dizer. Eu digo sempre o mesmo» ('No tengo nada nuevo que decir. Siempre digo lo mismo').

Eduardo Souto de Moura colecciona lo que encuentra y tiene una abundancia de fotografías, recortes de revistas y periódicos, que atesora sin más orden que el de la proximidad con algún proyecto que se esté realizando (imágenes de obras de Le Corbusier, Tessenow, Schinkel o Grassi al lado de un portaaviones, un puente o un búnker). Una vez usadas o revisadas, estas imágenes pasan a ser cuidadosamente guardadas. Algunas de esas fotografías o dibujos que aparecen y desaparecen de las paredes de su casa o de su estudio llegaron a configurar un libro, *Atlas de Parede. Imagens de Método*, en el que se muestra parte de esa labor de selección de imágenes para su uso. Es obvia una explicación de proximidad con otros atlas, especialmente el de Gerhard Richter y, por supuesto, el *Mnemosyne* de Aby Warburg. A pesar de esa tarea continuada de selección de imágenes, Souto prefirió elegir para este *Archives* veinticuatro retratos de aquellos «personajes» que ha ido seleccionando a lo largo de la historia y a través de las disciplinas que más necesita.

Lo que Eduardo ha seleccionado en esas 24 imágenes sin texto que aparecen en este *Archives* son su «*santinhos*», aquellas personas que con su trabajo, de verdad, le han modificado su forma de ver o de pensar, 24 retratos de escritores, músicos, arquitectos o escultores con un equilibrio numérico entre las distintas disciplinas.

El de Souto es un interés por el procedimiento que se muestra en mayor medida en esa relación tan fuerte con la literatura y que no solo le sirve para conocer procedimientos que pertenecen a la disciplina del escribir; también, entre otras cosas, para comprender el lugar en el que vive y mayoritariamente construye. Es necesario entender el territorio en donde uno vive. Portugal es un país pequeño cargado de historia que buscó a través de los mares la expansión que nace de una visión pragmática, con aspectos más cuantitativos que cualitativos, para crear una vasta red comercial. Esta relación de Portugal con el mundo fue teorizada por primera vez por Luís de Camões en *Os Lusíadas* y marca el nacimiento de la «adecuación» como identidad portuguesa, una adecuación que Eduardo toma como propia.

Souto defiende que en la arquitectura portuguesa siempre hubo un proceso de reelaboración por un desfase con los grandes centros de pensamiento. El poeta Paul Claudel escribió *«Portugal c'est un pays en voyage; de temps en temps il touche l'Europe»* ('Portugal es un país que está de viaje; de vez en cuando, toca Europa'). Este desfase lleva a un proceso de domesticación de las vanguardias que parte ya del Renacimiento y el Barroco y que más adelante, en el siglo XX, se confirma dentro de la arquitectura con la mirada a los márgenes del movimiento moderno que aportan Fernando Távora o Nuno Teotónio Pereira. También en el mirar a lo propio es necesario entender el movimiento de la Casa Portuguesa a finales del XIX, planteado como la formalización del léxico propuesto por Raul Lino y más adelante, a partir de 1955, la realización del *Inquérito à Arquitectura Popular em Portugal*, un conjunto de varios libros que contiene una extensa base documental para entender la arquitectura heredada de la tradición y así valorar ese proceso de adecuación, estableciendo adecuadamente una valoración ética de lo encontrado.

Távora es quien consigue ajustar el paso de la arquitectura portuguesa, estableciendo una relación crítica con la tradición, lo cotidiano, y con quien usa dicha arquitectura, en definitiva, con la vida que contiene. Ese encaje histórico de la arquitectura portuguesa con lo que sucedía fuera de sus fronteras parece acontecer en el momento adecuado, aunque Eduardo piense que mientras se dibujaban o se fotografiaban las casas y los *sequeiros* que se conservaban en las aldeas del interior de Portugal sucedía que Claude Lévi-Strauss o Michel Foucault escribían, en otros contextos, aspectos antropológicos y sociológicos mucho más interesantes. También Eduardo se queja de una interpretación posiblemente repetitiva y cerrada de lo recogido en el *Inquérito*, pero reconoce que es una pieza necesaria y fundamental que otros países no han llegado a formular y que hoy en día ya no podrían elaborar dada la desaparición de mucha arquitectura de la tradición que la *macdonalización* del planeta ha ido derribando. Mirando al *Inquérito*, Souto mira también hacia *A Casa Portuguesa* (1929) de Raul Lino a través de una lectura puntual que permite esa hibridación del uso de formas conocidas que propone.

El *Inquérito* es un esfuerzo de análisis y de generosidad, de la misma forma que también es relevante la implicación política de los arquitectos portugueses tras la Revolución de los Claveles. Desde fuera, parece que la arquitectura portuguesa ha sabido moverse de una forma más coordinada que en otros lugares y que la situación actual es fruto de ello.

Para Portugal (yo me atrevería a decir que para la arquitectura) ha sido muy importante la amistad y complicidad entre tres arquitectos, Távora, Siza y Souto, que acabarán compartiendo obras e incluso edificio para sus estudios. Esta es una maravillosa rareza que habla de cuán lejos están sus comportamientos de los habituales enfrentamientos entre arquitectos. Creo que buena parte del talante de la arquitectura portuguesa obedece a la trasmisión y alcance de esta circunstancia feliz. Tan solo se me ocurre comparar esta situación con la de los arquitectos Alejandro de la Sota, José Antonio Corrales, Ramón Vázquez Molezún y José María García de Paredes, a pocos pasos unos de otros en la calle Bretón de los Herreros, en Madrid, con buena relación y colaborando en algunos proyectos (también toca hoy en día revisar la vitalidad de la arquitectura que de allí surgió).

Estamos ante una búsqueda en lo próximo y en lo universal, con esa idea de *internacionalismo crítico* tal como la expone Jean-Louis Cohen. Cuando Souto realiza el proyecto del mercado de Braga y la intervención en una pequeña ruina en Gêres (1980), ya es consciente de que no era posible encontrar una cultura o un lenguaje puros, de que se estaba viviendo una etapa de transición. Un año más tarde, en 1981, gana el concurso para la Casa das Artes en Oporto y todo comienza a acelerarse.

Los proyectos de estos primeros años significan la aparición de buena parte de los elementos que definirán la arquitectura de Souto. Muchas de sus obras son viviendas, casas que constituyen un laboratorio en el que se van perfilando soluciones:

> Hay arquitectos que se pasan la vida diseñando siempre la misma casa. Hay arquitectos que se pasan la vida esperando al mismo cliente: ellos mismos.
>
> Desde «mi» primer proyecto, sigo diseñando la misma casa, como si se tratara de una obsesión. Aunque iguales, todas son diferentes, porque los lugares y las personas lo merecen.
>
> Siempre empiezo haciendo el proyecto de la misma casa, para la misma persona, pero con distintos seudónimos, y si fuera posible, como dice Aldo Rossi, «sin distraerme nunca con personas o casas que me parecen inútiles, considerando que el progreso en el arte

y en la ciencia depende de esta continuidad y constancia, las únicas cosas que permiten el cambio».[1]

Souto tiene muy claro que tiene que escribir sobre la casa, que tiene que formular aquello que a lo largo de su trabajo ha podido plantear, ensayar y comprobar.

En el año 1980, un minúsculo proyecto para la reconversión de una ruina en Gerês es el comienzo de su actividad constructora. Esta primera obra es una suerte de refugio en donde todo parece coincidir para llegar a un proyecto preciso y absolutamente necesario para iniciar el trabajo de Eduardo Souto de Moura. Se trata de un refugio en una ruina existente, con espacio para estar, dormir, un baño mínimo y una barra de cocina. Se conservaban todos los muros menos la zona que se ocupa con una gran ventana. Lo que desapareció, o lo que no tiene condiciones para permanecer, es sustituido por nuevos elementos, completamente ajenos a lo que allí existía: un forjado para hacer la cubierta y una losa para el suelo. La ruina se muestra deshaciéndose en todas partes y tras ella surge el vidrio, exacto y preciso.

Escribía Apollinaire que había que *«préparer au lierre et au temps une ruine plus belle que les autres...»* ('Preparar a la hiedra y a los tiempos una ruina más bella que las demás').[2] Un trabajo sobre la ruina como un estado de equilibrio entre la naturaleza y el artefacto. Un proyecto que, en resumen, busca la naturalidad. Una minúscula obra que parece predecir las voluntades que perseguirá Souto en numerosos proyectos.

Desde esta primera obra y a medida que va desarrollando su trabajo conserva una necesidad nostálgica de la memoria del lugar, del soporte físico sobre el que construye, una búsqueda que le lleva a la generación de contextos artificiales, de falsas ruinas, y, en términos generales, a la creación de nuevas líneas de continuidad.

Ruinas artificiales como las que realiza en la Casa 2 en Nevogilde (Oporto, 1983-1988) tras pasar tiempo dibujando en Roma.

La casa en Baião (1990-1993) es un proyecto posterior. En ella, conserva la ruina como jardín y se construye la casa al lado. La ruina aparece claramente definida y separada, como un objeto de contemplación. La casa se empotra en el terreno, con una única fachada totalmente acristalada.

En la casa en Moledo (1991), el programa de necesidades consiste en un listado convencional de habitaciones y, sin embargo, el lugar es muy exigente: una gran extensión de una empinada ladera con vistas al Atlántico, aterrazada mediante bancales agrícolas de una altura aproximada de 1,5 m. Rehacer las plataformas, con los muros de piedra para preparar un terreno propicio, fue lo que determinó todo el proyecto, y la casa es un tema menor en un conjunto muy potente topográficamente hablando, pero que

multiplica su relevancia al sumarse a la fuerza de una gran extensión de muros.

Como planteaba James S. Ackerman, la historia de la arquitectura occidental ha sido interpretada «entre los modos clásicos puristas y los pictóricos irregulares» y explicaba que esta batalla se podía ver perfectamente en lo que se conocía como *villa* que es una casa en un punto medio entre la vivienda urbana y la rural.[3] La tensión apuntada por Ackerman puede ser así ilustrada por la propia dirección que la obra de Souto de Moura ha seguido. Se diría que el clasicismo de la vía miesiana, que la casa en Moledo cristaliza, es gradualmente tomado por una torsión plástica, potencialmente pintoresca e ideológicamente no creyente...

El cambio se visualiza en la Casa do Cinema (1998-2003), pero va tomando forma en la casa en la sierra de Arrábida (1994-2002). En este proyecto, Souto cuenta cómo tras cuatro años superó las «crisis permanentes» y las dificultades personales de definición de un lenguaje. El problema residía en que la adecuación de cualquier experiencia anterior a este proyecto no era compatible ni con el cliente, ni con la topografía, ni «conmigo mismo»:

> Frente al incremento de la complejidad, necesitamos más que nunca un pensamiento simplificador, pero que no sea mutilador. Cuando la realidad se resista a la simplificación,

> tenemos que volver a la complejidad. La complejidad es la irrupción del desorden de lo aleatorio y de la incertidumbre en la realidad... Hoy todos sabemos que el futuro es incierto dada la perpetua intervención de la novedad y de lo imprevisto. Por eso la complejidad extrema tiende a parecerse a una crisis permanente.[4]

El tránsito entre modos clásicos puristas y los pictóricos irregulares parece no obedecer en el caso de Eduardo a cambios debidos a una evolución personal; más bien, podría hablarse de una concatenación de situaciones encontradas en las que va resolviendo proyectos que modifican o reformulan planteamientos pretéritos.

Souto realizaba casas generalmente de una sola planta, muy adaptadas al terreno y a sus límites, que en Portugal siempre se marcan con muros con gran presencia y de una forma excepcional en los bancales del Duero o en los muros de piedra que separan las bodegas de Vilanova de Gaia. En la obra de Souto, los muros participan con la casa y esto le lleva a trabajar con patios de una u otra forma: en las casas de Matosinhos, las de Pasteleira...

Se trata de largos muros que muestran su constitución en las esquinas, con las superficies acristaladas concentradas y generosas en sus dimensiones. La ventana en los primeros proyectos de Souto no existía como tal: tan solo trabajaba con la diferenciación entre positivo y negativo, muro y vidrio. No necesitaba componer las ventanas; las zonas cerradas o abiertas aparecían de forma natural. A partir de la casa en Tavira aparece la ventana y su composición hasta llegar a proyectos únicamente de ventanas como las del conjunto de Santa Coloma de Gramenet.

Además de las casas, algún otro proyecto se va enhebrando desde el comienzo. La Casa das Artes de Oporto (1981) muestra un Souto claro en la organización del programa y atento al detalle para disimular elementos que molestan en la búsqueda de la abstracción: estores, carpinterías... Esta labor que inicia tiene un recorrido amplio en el tiempo y en los proyectos; se desenvuelve en el trabajo para llegar a lo esencial. Esta búsqueda se transmite magníficamente a través de la poesía. Souto siempre encuentra un momento para referirse a los poemas de Herberto Helder, un poeta escondido, reacio a que se le conociese y se le reconociese, y que apenas ha sido traducido a otros idiomas por culpa de su infranqueable modestia.

> Qualquer poema é um filme, e o único elemento que importa é o tempo, e o espaço é a metáfora do tempo, e o que se narra é a ressurreição do instante exatamente anterior à morte, a fulgurante agonia de um nervo que irrompe do poema e faz saltar a vida dentro da massa irreal do mundo. [...] A poesia propõe a história do mundo. Temos então o filme, o tempo.[5]

Si volvemos a la reconversión de la ruina en Gerês, podemos observar con detenimiento los dibujos de planta y sección del proyecto, comenzando con ese trabajo constante en la definición de cómo construye. La posición de la carpintería está adelantada con respecto al volumen, superponiéndose al plano del forjado superior. Sin embargo, la solución finalmente ejecutada contiene la carpintería entre el plano de forjado y el del suelo. Este juego se proyecta ocultando el plano de la estructura con el vidrio y en otros casos se busca la evidencia de la estructura de una forma clara. La relación entre las superficies acristaladas y las estructuras constituye un trabajo que se va alternando entre obras e incluso dentro de la misma, como sucede en la Casa 2 en Nevogilde, donde encontramos numerosas soluciones de lo que ocurre con las zonas acristaladas y sus relaciones con lo que las rodea.

En continuidad con varias casas, el Espaço Miguel Torga es un proyecto del año 2007 que continúa investigaciones anteriores de proyectos de viviendas o el de la Casa das Artes. Está definido por muros que delimitan el espacio interior y se expanden más allá de lo cubierto para cerrar la parcela. Grandes losas de esquisto en vertical, al igual que se colocan para los cierres de algunas fincas, son la imagen potente que muestra la magnitud de su espesor en los cortes de los muros. Los huecos aparecen únicamente en los puntos necesarios, ocultando estructuras y falsos techos.

El vidrio permite la superposición, el reflejo, la transparencia, la disolución del límite, la evidencia del espesor o bien su ocultamiento, procesos que aparecen de una forma pautada en sus proyectos, como si no quisiese abandonarlos.

En el juego del reflejo y la transparencia, hay un proyecto especial, el de Pabellón de Portugal en la 11.ª Bienal de Arquitectura de Venecia del año 2008: una fachada totalmente acristalada, con vidrio que actúa como espejo de la vida que sucede en el gran canal y de los edificios que se encuentran enfrente. Este proyecto, realizado con Ângelo de Sousa, sobresale con respecto a la dimensión real del almacén sobre el que actúan hasta alcanzar la altura de la casa vecina, un proyecto pensado por alguien que conoce a Venturi y a Dan Graham.

En la obra de Souto hay una insistencia en la ocultación de ciertas realidades, especialmente de las estructuras horizontales, y normalmente motivada por la persecución de una ansiada ligereza y de la elegancia. Los encuentros para mostrar o bien ocultar se desarrollan según los proyectos y esto se concreta en esa zona de contacto entre el exterior y el interior. La sección es una herramienta clara para averiguar los matices que desde el exterior pueden percibirse. La sección a partir de ese punto inicial se convierte en uniforme con pocas opciones de acompañar a la volumetría del edificio. El Paula Rego (2005-2009) es de los pocos proyectos en los que se rompe el paralelismo entre el plano del suelo y el del techo al aparecer esas grandes *chimeneas*, y sorprende que en el multiusos de Viana do Castelo (2000-2013) no se haya optado por esconder la estructura.

Resulta muy clara su defensa de la belleza, ya que asegura que la imagen o la forma funciona antes que el contenido. Cuestiona la necesidad de la verdad en la arquitectura frente al truco para conseguir la belleza y en ese análisis de lo que practica en sus obras busca el apoyo de la filosofía o de la literatura: *La historia de la mentira* de Jacques Derrida, *La mentira* de San Agustín o *Sobre la decadencia del arte de mentir* de Mark Twain.

Sus proyectos no esconden la creación de la «mentira» necesaria: lo que le preocupa es crear un sistema que parezca auténtico, conseguir una coherencia que pueda ser construida, y le interesa, en menor grado, la autenticidad misma.

Sin embargo, sus puentes y sus escaleras carecen de argucias: son claros y directos, sin ocultar las partes o los elementos que usa. El proyecto de puente de la Academia que realiza para el concurso que organiza la Bienal de Venecia del año 1985 o el puente sobre el 24 de Julio en Lisboa, al igual que cualquiera de sus escaleras, presentan un alto grado de precisión (pensemos en la temprana escalera de la Casa das Artes o la reciente del auditorio de Portalegre de 2009). Una escalera, aunque no propia, se convierte en protagonista del proyecto del pabellón para la Trienal de Milán del año 2016. Souto construye una gran caja para transportar obras de arte, dispuesta para recibir la pieza del artista Jannis Kounellis (una escalera): una caja al exterior con sus refuerzos y al interior sin juntas y con el color que eligió el artista para destacar la pieza.

Hace suya una frase de Rafael Moneo, según la que, en el proyecto, al principio, todas las decisiones son arbitrarias, pero nuestra obligación es darles un sentido a esas arbitrariedades. Souto añade que lo más importante es la coherencia en el proceso, en el desarrollo de cada proyecto. El problema estriba en que cuanto más simple se muestra una imagen, más tortuosa ha sido su construcción. Cuanto más complejo es el resultado, más descuidado ha sido el diseño. El punto exacto está en la vigilia, en la mutación periódica, como en las estaciones del año.

La realidad en la que estamos inmersos, la realidad de la arquitectura, rechaza la simplicidad y sostiene que hay que afrontar la complejidad, esa complejidad que va anudando sus proyectos.

Las referencias a la escala son evidentes y se maneja bien con ella. Sus edificios encuentran esa escala adecuada.

Suele aparecer una cierta ironía en sus proyectos, y en algunos lo hace de una forma muy evidente, como en las dos casas en Ponte da Lima (2001-2002). Son dos casas y un único programa: una se resuelve pegada al terreno y la otra despegándose del suelo, casi flotando; dos casas que no tienen sentido separadas y que tan solo se pueden entender de forma conjunta.

Más tarde, otro juego de dos casas, en esta ocasión en el Duero (2004), que obedecen a juegos distintos: una es el cruce de dos volúmenes prismáticos girados noventa grados que se apoyan en el núcleo de comunicaciones y la otra es una casa invertida que resulta de girarla totalmente, para que lo que equivaldría a la cubierta sea lo que se apoya en el terreno.

Estos giros también se suceden con respecto al plano del terreno, y de ahí la insistencia en los cubos girados que sirven para el proyecto de la Iglesia de la Misericordia (1998) o para el café del Eixo Deportivo Braga (1983).

Juegos puntuales como la exageración de la máquina en el pabellón multiusos de Viana do Castelo o la mirada sin complejos de un silo para convertirse en el auditorio de Portalegre.

Pocos son los arquitectos que tienen que intervenir sobre proyectos suyos pretéritos. En el caso de Souto, esta circunstancia es doble: por un lado, el mercado de Braga (1980) que, tras su derribo parcial (en el que se exhiben parte de sus ruinas), llega a configurar un nuevo espacio cultural con un cambio muy significativo con respecto al proyecto inicial; por otro, la casa en Quinta do Lago (1984) también requiere su intervención con la llegada de un nuevo propietario que necesita aumentar su superficie. El proyecto de Souto para esta casa consiste en un proceso de estiramiento del conjunto para alcanzar ese aumento de superficie, consiguiendo como resultado una mayor ligereza en la estructura.

Las ironías llegan hasta el momento actual, cuando en A Caida (2009-2019) forra una construcción existente, descuidada, realizada con ladrillo, sin acabar, y lo hace con más ladrillo, pero colocado con toda la precisión posible.

A Caida presenta una propuesta unificadora de lo encontrado (con la excepción de una construcción separada del conjunto principal). Esta unificación se consigue con la aplicación de una capa protectora a todos los cerramientos. El proceso de A Caida es similar al de la reconversión del Convento das Bernardas (2006-2012) en donde esa capa protectora unifica la imagen exterior de unos muros muy alterados antes y en la obra.

Por último, el proyecto de la Torre Burgo, un edificio de oficinas en la avenida de Boavista-Burgo en Oporto, que quedó paralizado en la crisis de los noventa y no llegó a construirse hasta el año 2007. De

la imagen inicial tomada de referencia de un apilamiento de materiales habituales en la construcción, pasó a ser el edificio y, su maqueta, un mueble-bar doméstico.

Una de las obras más conocidas de Eduardo Souto es la intervención en el monasterio de Santa María de Bouro (1989-1997), un proyecto que quiere conservar el aspecto de ruina en el monasterio que conocía de sus estancias infantiles. Esa ruina que podría llegar desde la lectura de Ruskin, frente a una interpretación más próxima a Viollet le Duc de los últimos años. En los últimos proyectos (especialmente en A Caida) intenta recomponer una realidad imaginada que no había sucedido antes de intervenir Souto.

En el año 2000, Souto comienza a trabajar en la reconversión del Sanatório dos Ferroviários en Covilha, un edificio de 1944 que se había ido degradando hasta convertirse en una ruina: el proyecto de transformar estas ruinas en un hotel y balneario le lleva a afianzar los elementos que se conservan para conseguir, de nuevo, el mismo ambiente que tenía el edificio sin que genere en quien lo vea una sensación de extrañeza con huellas de otro momento distinto al de su creación. En el Sanatório dos Ferroviários desarolla un ejercicio de contención para evitar interferencias con el proyecto original.

Unos años más tarde, en 2008, comienza el proyecto en São Lourenço do Barrocal para convertirlo en un complejo turístico. Es una intervención extremadamente respetuosa que ante todo prioriza conservar un conjunto edificado excepcional. Frente a los habituales planteamientos de conservación de edificios para contenidos culturales, el planteamiento de Barrocal es el de ser consciente de que la única manera de preservar el patrimonio es vivir con él y usarlo, incluso si está dañado en algunos lugares.

El funcionamiento de Barrocal como hotel es preciso y exacto, y uno parece encontrarse cómodo, sin estridencias y disonancias. Sucede algo similar en la intervención en los espacios públicos en Valença (2003). En Valença cuesta encontrar la mano de Eduardo; parece estar realizado por una mano ágil e inteligente y se agradece esta desaparición del autor en un núcleo urbano tan característico.

Es en el proyecto de A Caida, que todavía está sin finalizar en este momento, en el que más abunda en la reconfiguración de lo encontrado para conseguir un conjunto con unidad. Con referencias muy claras a la arquitectura anónima y más en concreto en aquella que está a pocos kilómetros, A Caida es toda una suerte de investigación en la que se está adentrando en este momento en el que es necesario redefinir cuál debe ser nuestro comportamiento frente a situaciones en las que los conjuntos edificados necesitan adecuación y no disonancias propias de egos arquitectónicos variados. Frente a la mirada a la arquitectura anónima que se muestra en la casa en Quinta do Lago que le sirve para definir volúmenes que posa sobre el plano de cubierta (cúpula, pirámide), esta revisión que está realizando en este momento le sirve para solucionar huecos, esquinas, vuelos y cambios de plano. Ojalá pueda encontrarse Souto con más situaciones como la de A Caida para seguir analizando en un terreno extraordinariamente interesante y oportuno.

Souto reconoce que es un trabajador incansable. La poeta Sophia de Mello escribió que a ella la poesía le pedía una «obstinación densa y compacta». La pasión junto con la obstinación o la constancia de Eduardo, junto con la continuidad, resume su trabajo. Souto de Moura habla de la adecuación de la disciplina a la cultura y al lugar para buscar los motivos para pensar, escribir y edificar. Todo con pasión. Como escribía Herberto Helder en *A Paixão Grega*:[6]

> Li algures que os gregos antigos não
> [escreviam necrológios,
> quando alguém morria perguntavam apenas:
> tinha paixão?
> quando alguém morre também eu quero saber
> [da qualidade da sua paixão:
> se tinha paixão pelas coisas gerais,
> água,
> música,
> pelo talento de algumas palavras para
> [se moverem no caos,

pelo corpo salvo dos seus precipícios
[com destino à glória,
paixão pela paixão,
tinha?
e então indago de mim se eu próprio
[tenho paixão,
se posso morrer gregamente,
que paixão?

Una pasión que no distingue entre lo pequeño y lo grande. La selección de obras de este número de *Archives* ha buscado la reunión de proyectos de tamaño mínimo como la capilla en Venecia y de otros de escala territorial como la presa. La facilidad que ha demostrado en intervenciones de gran tamaño como el metro de Oporto son ejemplos magníficos de control total del proyecto y de cómo la reducción a reglas muy sencillas es determinante, por ejemplo, la repetición en la dimensión de la piedra utilizada puede llevar a la unidad y coherencia del resultado final, al mismo tiempo que mejora su economía. Sin embargo, por otro lado, conviene mirar con el mayor de los intereses sus proyectos de menor tamaño: el primero en la ruina del Gêres y el último de la capilla en Venecia. Ambos proyectos son excepcionales: la ruina inicia una buena etapa en sus primeros años y la capilla no solo se configura como un proyecto excepcional de Souto, sino que también muestra unas posibilidades de expresión sincera que aventura magníficos proyectos futuros.

1. Eduardo Souto de Moura, 7 de marzo de 1989.
2. Apollinaire, *Les Peintres cubistes. Méditations esthétiques*, 1913.
3. James S. Ackerman: *La villa. Forma e ideología de las casas de campo* [Madrid: Akal], 1997. Traducción de I. Balsinde.
4. De la memoria de la casa en Arrábida.
5. Herberto Helder: *Photomaton & Vox* [Lisboa: Assírio & Alvim], 2006, 140.
6.Herberto Helder: «A Paixão Grega», en *A Faca não Corta o Fogo* [Lisboa: Assírio & Alvim], 2008, 612.

Capilla del Vaticano

Isla de San Giorgio Maggiore, Venecia (Italia) 2018

No, no es una capilla, no es un santuario, pero tampoco es un túmulo. Es un espacio cerrado por muros de piedra, con un altar situado en la zona más amplia y alejada de la entrada. Una cubierta tapa parcialmente el recinto y se sitúa sobre las piedras hincadas en el terreno. La entrada está situada en relación con un árbol existente. Los muros hacia el interior tienen una segunda piedra que sirve de asiento y apoyo para cualquier ceremonia. Un banco para «sentarse y esperar... esperar con los pies en la tierra y la cabeza en las manos» (David Mourão Ferreira).

Convento de las Bernardas

Tavira (Portugal) 2006–2012

El Convento de las Bernardas fue fundado por el Císter en 1509 en la ciudad de Tavira. Dañado por el terremoto de Lisboa, sufrió varias reformas hasta que en 1834 se convirtió en fábrica para quedar luego en abandono y pasar a ser una ruina. Por lo general, el uso de estas ruinas está asociado a programas de hoteles, museos o centros culturales, pero no existe una viabilidad económica para tantos objetos disponibles.

Se ha optado por la conversión del convento en un complejo residencial, con una adaptación funcional de lo existente, rehabilitando lo que todavía era posible mantener y procurando corregir errores del pasado. El complejo consta de viviendas de diferentes tamaños que se integran en la estructura existente y en un cuerpo nuevo orientado al este que aprovecha el desnivel que existía entre la plataforma superior y el nivel en el que se situaba el antiguo huerto.

En el cuerpo de la iglesia, que ya había sido dividido en tres secciones, la nave central se vuelve a utilizar como zona de recepción, y se propone una cafetería en la sacristía y otras salas. La estructura existente de la torre se usa para acomodar cuatro casas de distintos tamaños que se adaptan a la geometría irregular de los muros.

Dentro del resto de los muros existentes del convento, las viviendas se distribuyen en módulos independientes en tres alturas.

El Convento de las Bernardas es el resultado de sucesivas intervenciones de ampliación y prolongación en la construcción original. En todos los muros se contempló el aprovechamiento de los huecos existentes, la reapertura de ventanas que se encontraban cerradas y la apertura de nuevas ventanas y puertas, multiplicando así los huecos. El nuevo edificio está semienterrado, en forma de «L», en el tramo oriental, y formado por una línea de casas unifamiliares en una o dos plantas con terrazas en lo que fue la huerta del convento. Las casas de este nuevo cuerpo miran hacia las salinas que las rodean al igual que las otras viviendas lo hacen hacia la piscina de agua salada situada en el gran patio central.

Todo el conjunto se pinta para unificar los muros de distinto tipo, los huecos y las huellas que estos han generado. La vegetación cobra protagonismo, conservando las palmeras, añadiendo los árboles en el patio central y con las trepadoras en los muros. Unas pérgolas metálicas con vegetación generan sombra a las viviendas y ayudan a ocultar coches e instalaciones.

São Lourenço do Barrocal

Reguengos de Monsaraz (Portugal) 2008–2016

São Lourenço do Barrocal es una finca que creció en el XIX hasta convertirse en una pequeña aldea que tiene su propia jerarquía: una calle, una plaza, dependencias, claustros. Se trata de un conjunto que rara vez se encuentra en tan buenas condiciones. Situado en un paisaje del Alentejo, formado por encinas, viñedos y olivares, el núcleo está caracterizado por siete edificios dispuestos a lo largo de una calle central que define dos conjuntos principales (Norte y Sur). El complejo Norte constaba de dos edificios: el antiguo edificio industrial y de oficina, y el almacén de las herramientas agrícolas. El complejo Sur tenía cinco edificios: la casa principal, los pabellones agrícolas, la pajarera, la perrera y la porqueriza. Más al sur se encuentra la zona de huerta y la piscina al aire libre que conserva un afloramiento de granito *(barrocal)*.

El proyecto de transformación de este conjunto en un complejo turístico trata de encontrar el equilibrio entre lo existente y el ajuste a la nueva situación. Cada una de las edificaciones se adapta al nuevo programa con pequeñas modificaciones, siendo consciente de que la única forma de conservar el patrimonio es usándolo.instalaciones.

Escuela de Hostelería y Turismo & Fundación Robinson

En colaboración con Graça Correia. Portalegre (Portugal) 2004–2009

El traslado de la Fábrica de Corcho Robinson a la nueva zona industrial de Portalegre generó un vacío de casi 60 000 m² en una importante área de desarrollo metropolitano de la ciudad, un área construida con hangares, almacenes y talleres, además del edificio principal que define su frente. El programa de rehabilitación de las instalaciones de la antigua fábrica busca recuperar su conexión histórica con la ciudad, redefiniendo las funciones de varios edificios y recuperando un notable patrimonio industrial. El plan introduce plazas, paseos y equipamientos, permitiendo la articulación entre los edificios de la Fábrica Robinson y el tejido urbano existente, todo esto marcado físicamente por el rasgado correspondiente a la apertura de una calle.

La ocupación está destinada a garantizar la supervivencia de la implantación original con las sucesivas y necesarias ampliaciones que se llevarán a cabo partiendo de un principio aditivo que ordena todo el conjunto industrial. Este, formado por los edificios ya dispuestos a lo largo de una especie de camino, configura ahora una nueva relación con el entorno mediante la implantación estratégica de los nuevos edificios de la Escuela de Hostelería y un primer auditorio, que contribuirá a la definición clara de una calle entendida en su forma urbana.

Dentro del plan, la ubicación del estacionamiento es fundamental. La estructura permite la realización de otras actividades diferentes a las de aparcamiento.

El auditorio cumple la doble función de cerrar la línea de construcciones adaptadas para el Centro Internacional de Realidad Virtual (TIC-VR) y de un segundo auditorio, y, al mismo tiempo, crea una referencia en el trayecto de la calle. Es un equipo esencialmente de apoyo a la Escuela de Hostelería y Turismo que funciona en convivencia con el segundo auditorio. Uno de los supuestos del plan es la utilización compartida de las infraestructuras. El auditorio fue pensado con un sistema constructivo y una imagen de «máquina metálica»: una escultura que marca su presencia dentro del conjunto fabril.

Al sur, el edificio de la Escuela de Hostelería y Turismo está pensado como una caja que se apoya sobre el terreno, definiendo un gran balcón al que se abren todos los espacios principales de la escuela a la vez (clases, biblioteca, zona de estar, restaurante y bar). Al norte, la caja está cerrada hacia la calle.

La propuesta de todo el conjunto asume un riesgo al pretender corregir la situación crítica de desorden en el crecimiento urbano actual de Portalegre, revalorizando sus recursos y potencialidades. En la estrategia de implantación de los nuevos edificios se consideró el recurso del elemento iconográfico presente en la memoria común: la silueta de las chimeneas que se destaca en el perfil de la ciudad.

Espaço Miguel Torga

Sabrosa (Portugal) 2007–2011

El Centro Cultural Espaço Miguel Torga se usa para estudiar y difundir la obra poética y literaria de Miguel Torga. Está emplazado al sur de un antiguo recinto ferial, situado cerca de la casa natal del poeta y rodeado por dos vías longitudinales que convergen. El edificio toca ambas vías y se sitúa entre dos espacios de características diferentes: al norte una zona asfaltada en la que se celebran las ferias cada dos semanas y al sur un viñedo. Hacia el norte se han colocado 35 árboles que forman una malla que a su vez ordena el mercado, así como el aparcamiento en el resto de los días.

El edificio está definido por muros de esquistos (elemento característico de esta zona) que definen los límites de lo construido y del espacio próximo, configurando totalmente su imagen. Aprovecha la pendiente del terreno y los muros se extienden hacia el norte para delimitar el recinto ferial; por la pendiente de terreno, los muros reducen su altura hasta convertirse en bancos.

Cuenta con dos accesos, uno público (al este) y otro de servicio (al oeste), definidos por un desencuentro entre las paredes.

La entrada principal da acceso a la sala de exposiciones, detrás de la cual se ubica la zona de biblioteca, despachos de administración y salas de estudio. La iluminación de estas piezas se realiza a través de una serie de patios privados que quedan ocultos tras el muro de la fachada norte del edificio. La cafetería tiene una fachada de vidrio (la única que se percibe desde el exterior) con una entrada directa para un funcionamiento independiente.

Pabellón multiusos

Viana do Castelo (Portugal) 2000–2013

El pabellón multiusos de Viana do Castelo está en la desembocadura del río Lima, situado junto a la biblioteca de Álvaro Siza y alineado con el edificio destinado a centro de ocio de Fernando Távora, en una zona privilegiada de la orilla del río. Una zona arbolada se coloca frente al alzado noroeste; con alamedas se marca el acceso al pabellón y una rampa a la planta -1. Los principales accesos se sitúan en las fachadas noroeste y sureste.

Formalmente, el edificio se define como una mesa sobre la que se apoya una caja de aluminio y todos los equipamientos necesarios para el funcionamiento de las actividades culturales, musicales, deportivas y de ocio que se desarrollan en su interior. Con capacidad para 4000 personas, el nuevo edificio tiene una superficie de 3792 m² repartidos en tres plantas. En la planta -1 se encuentra la pista y el acceso a los graderíos laterales. En el nivel 0, un deambulatorio utiliza el vidrio para garantizar la transparencia entre la ciudad, el río y el interior del edificio. Por último, en la planta 1 se encuentran las cabinas de control y los espacios administrativos.

Se trata de un edificio cuya imagen industrial o naval evoca la del antiguo buque-hospital Gil Eannes que se encuentra amarrado como barco museo en el puerto de la localidad.

Presa Foz Tua

Alijó, Douro (Portugal) 2011–2018

La principal preocupación del proyecto era minimizar el impacto visual de la presa, conseguir la mayor integración posible y eliminar el carácter de edificio en esta construcción casi enteramente subterránea que adopta formas y materiales característicos de la región, buscando mostrarse como una «máquina» colocada en el paisaje. Todo el proyecto ha procurado minimizar las alteraciones morfológicas de las vertientes y compactar lo construido para reducir la volumetría expuesta de las obras y su impacto visual.

En la base de la montaña encontramos el edificio técnico de la central, construido en terrazas y cubierto con tierra vegetal para dar continuidad y remate al corte realizado. Este edificio solo es visible por algunos cajones de hormigón con los accesos y las salidas de ventilación. Una plataforma en hormigón cubre el gran atrio enterrado y los pozos en donde se sitúan los sistemas reversibles de turbina-bombeo. Sobre la plataforma existe una grúa pórtico, los transformadores..., aquellos elementos que necesariamente debían estar al aire libre, colocados de la forma más concentrada posible. Para realizar esta plataforma de 36 m de ancho, fue necesario practicar un corte de 45° en la montaña. Para conseguir la forma final más natural posible se cortó la roca y se fijó con una red metálica casi imperceptible, evitando el uso de muros de hormigón para la contención. En esta pendiente serán plantados olivos para conseguir una continuidad con los terrenos próximos.

El edificio social está enterrado bajo la plataforma principal, entre los dos cilindros que contienen los motores auxiliares; al exterior queda visible únicamente una línea de 25 m por un metro de altura para dar luz y ventilación al programa: centro de control, salas de reuniones, vestuarios, servicios...
Una caja de vidrio para el puesto de observación y un depósito de agua con forma de cono invertido, realizado en hormigón, contrastan con la riqueza natural del entorno.

Casa Quinta do Lago

Algarve (Portugal) 2015–2017

Este es un proyecto con dos etapas. La primera nace en 1984 cuando se proyecta y construye esta casa de vacaciones en el Algarve junto a un campo de golf. Con reglas muy claras, impuestas por la urbanización, la casa surgió como un paralelepípedo apoyado en el césped. El proyecto inicial nace del cruce de la arquitectura popular del sur de Portugal con algunas casas chinas (realizó el proyecto en Macau). No es indiferente a las obras previas de Souto y contiene miradas hacia la obra de Le Corbusier.

Pasadas tres décadas, un nuevo propietario quiere aumentar sus dimensiones con una cocina mayor, una sala de estar más dimensionada, con comedor, una suite independiente y un espacio para guardar como mínimo cuatro coches.

Para conseguir dar respuesta a las nuevas condiciones y ante la obligación de conservar el edificio, el proyecto aumenta el volumen conservando todas las características, «estirando» el edificio y consiguiendo una proporción en el conjunto más ligera. Se mantienen las razones originales con las que nació el edificio. Parte del programa va bajo tierra, de modo que los coches y zonas de almacenaje se sitúan en un sótano con acceso por ascensor, desapareciendo así su presencia en el exterior cuando no están en uso.

A Caida

Quinta da Caida-Arcas. Macedo de Cavaleiros (Portugal) 2009–2019

A Caida era un pequeño núcleo abandonado de cinco edificaciones en un considerable estado de degradación que presentaba un carácter más uniforme en el conjunto principal formado por cuatro edificios y un estilo diferenciado en la construcción aislada de una antigua vaquería. Todos ellos contienen características reconocibles de distintos momentos de una arquitectura anónima.

Conservando todo lo edificado, se le añade un nuevo edificio para aumentar las unidades de alojamiento y conseguir la viabilidad económica de la propuesta. Este nuevo edificio está planteado como otro muro de piedra colocado para resolver un cambio de cota del terreno y minimizando con su disposición la destrucción del revestimiento vegetal.

Tres edificios son de alojamiento, próximos a un edificio de apoyo que también hará de recepción. La antigua vaquería, aislada, se usa como vivienda de los cuidadores del conjunto y de la explotación agrícola.

Se conservan las volumetrías existentes adoptando las metodologías de construcción tradicional característica de esta zona. Se mantienen los materiales existentes y se busca conseguir unidad al cubrir todos los muros de piedra de una protección impermeabilizante y dignificar la construcción aislada de la antigua vaquería con el ladrillo más cuidado posible.

Algunos de los puntos clave de un proyecto que siempre mira a lo existente en las aldeas próximas y que lo dignifica a través de operaciones muy sencillas vinculadas al detalle, los espesores y los materiales son la consolidación de los muros, los nuevos pavimentos de grandes espesores, las aperturas adecuadas de los huecos y las chimeneas proyectadas desde una visión plástica de conjunto.
A Caida es una operación delicada que elimina la presencia de una autoría reconocible y que contiene una mirada sincera hacia la necesaria intervención en todo aquello que la precariedad y la inmediatez han ido dejando en la mayor parte del territorio rural de Portugal.

Pedro Cabrita Reis

Carlos Quintáns

Pedro Cabrita llega a su taller con los restos de algo quemado que ha encontrado en la calle. Algunas piezas metálicas sobresalen en un conjunto que debió estar fluido y que adoptó la forma del suelo sobre el que se apoyó y la discontinuidad de lo que pudo ir cayendo mientras ardía. Una masa informe que ha llegado circunstancialmente a una forma «adecuada» para ser usada en cualquier momento en la obra de Cabrita. Una pieza que se deja caer cerca de otras muchas que ya han sido usadas: puertas, ventanas, vidrios, sillas... Todo perfectamente ordenado.

El taller de Cabrita es un antiguo almacén dentro de un gran edificio. Las ventanas que dan a la calle interior de este conjunto permiten ver una enorme zona en la que conviven muchas de sus obras tras una puerta que reza «a revolução sou eu».[1] Una planta más arriba, la zona en donde se preparan y elaboran las piezas, y un despacho ligeramente elevado. Una planta más alta, la casa a la que se llega al pasar un volumen absolutamente blanco, con una escalera que la separa de la zona de trabajo. La casa permite una visión longitudinal libre al igual que en las otras dos plantas, con enormes espacios y unos muebles maravillosos dispuestos a ser usados o solamente contemplados.

Comenzamos la conversación en su despacho, frente a sus libros (los otros los guarda en su casa cerca de Tavira). Cada cierto tiempo se va deshaciendo de algunos para conservar únicamente aquellos que tienen que ver con el trabajo y que se van filtrando. Libros que le van apoyando en el conocimiento que tiene de sí mismo. Confiesa que esta «limpieza» proviene de alguien al que le gusta proyectarse en el futuro y que prefiere tener una memoria frágil.

No tiene problemas en trabajar con gente que viene a verle. El taller es un lugar de reunión, un lugar al que se acercan: unos hablan, otros hacen... Aquí no hay silencio; el silencio es interior. No hay rechazo. Su taller es un lugar de convergencia, una fábrica de pensamiento en la que no hay modelos.

En el año 2021 espera que se pueda inaugurar su fundación con un proyecto de Eduardo Souto de Moura, aunque es pronto para hablar de ello. Con Eduardo tan solo ha coincidido trabajando en el crematorio en Cortrique, en Bélgica, en el edificio para Novartis en Basel y en la exposición «D'après Fibonacci e as coisas lá fora» de Jorge Pinheiro en la fundación Serralves. No necesitan más; se encuentran, se observan, hablan. No es una relación continuada, pero cuando se encuentran tiene la sensación

de continuar su última conversación. La suya es una relación intensa de proyecto y pensamiento.

Para Pedro, Eduardo es una persona única con un pensamiento claro, con una obra que vive por sí misma. Le interesa Eduardo como hombre que piensa, el filósofo, el poeta, con el que tiene una afinidad electiva, volviendo a Kant. Le resulta atractiva su mirada sobre el mundo, una mirada que interroga, y le interesan sus dibujos con los que quiere transformar el mundo.

Pedro habla con contundencia, sin dudar, de forma categórica. Es tan claro que parece que ha preparado su conversación para que pueda transcribirse literalmente.

El trabajo de Cabrita es también muy claro y hay una percepción de que tiene una mirada muy próxima a la arquitectura, pero en realidad la arquitectura no le interesa. Le interesa el acto de la construcción. Sus programas son diferentes, con puntos de contacto y un pensamiento que es coincidente.

El arquitecto, al mirar el contexto, lo observa de la misma manera en la que el artista mira el del pensamiento en el que se encuentra. La arquitectura es un dispositivo intelectual que tiene que ver con la gestión política del espacio, sea privado o público. La arquitectura es la respuesta de la humanidad a vivir juntos para diseñar la política de convivencia que es lo que le interesa.

Un artista no tiene que dar respuesta a una pregunta, a una propuesta basada en la realidad; nace de un imaginario que surge de la realidad. No hay arte fuera de la realidad. No hay arte fuera de un pensamiento crítico.

El arte abstracto es tan abstracto como un autorretrato del siglo XV o XVI. No hay arte abstracto: hay respuestas a estímulos, a circunstancias a contextos históricos, filosóficos, políticos, poéticos, de índole narrativa, más abstracta o filosófica.

A Cabrita como artista le preocupa una antropología filosófica de la relación del individuo con la naturaleza: el acto de poner una piedra sobre otra piedra y con eso construir un territorio.

La humanidad construye su propia naturaleza en cuanto especie humana sobre la naturaleza encontrada que sirve de territorio de ocupación. El arte busca imaginar y reproducir las distintas posibilidades de relación del individuo con su contexto natural, entendiendo que además puede cambiar la percepción que los hombres tienen de todo e incluso de sí mismos.

No le parece interesante reivindicar una autoría, prefiere hablar de buscar para cada uno un estatuto, una posición de curiosidad y, con eso, construir una nueva narrativa.

La conversación con Pedro Cabrita es larga e intensa, la de alguien que no esconde su pensamiento y del que brota una vitalidad contagiosa.

Era necesario algo más que un texto y Pedro consigue que en el restaurante le impriman una imagen de su última obra. Sobre ella dibuja dos chimeneas con lápiz, al que añade con su mano restos del vino tinto de la cena. Eduardo & Cabrita.

1. 'La revolución soy yo'.

Continuidad, esquinas y bricolaje en la arquitectura de Souto de Moura

Santiago de Molina

I.

Treinta mil personas vitorean la salida al campo del Sporting Clube de Braga cada partido. La multitud anima mientras el estadio, conocido popularmente entre los aficionados como «A Pedreira» ('La cantera'), retumba como un inmenso espectador más debido al eco que produce el monumental cortado de piedra de la montaña próxima.

Indudablemente, ese muro de piedra permanece ajeno al resultado del acontecimiento deportivo de turno, al igual que el ciego estadio de hormigón que lo abraza. Sin embargo, la multitud abandonará lentamente ese espacio, de vuelta a la ciudad, descendiendo primero por las gradas, luego por las mil escaleras interiores, caminando entre las costillas de ese grandioso animal de hormigón hueco, felices o pesarosos en función del siempre incierto resultado. El estadio, de una dureza intransigente, aparentemente mudo y colosal, volverá una semana más a ser espacio vacío a la espera de un nuevo evento. Sin embargo, puede que el adormecimiento solo sea aparente, porque el estadio vive dentro de un sistema rítmico de otro orden, de otro tiempo, capaz de aunar partidos semanales con la eternidad mineral de la roca misma sobre la que se apoya.

Si hubiese que hacer un análisis cabal de la obra del estadio de Braga, no podría pasarse por alto cómo actúa en él un sentido del tiempo externo a lo cotidiano semejante al descrito más arriba, hasta tal punto que se podría afirmar que se trata de una infraestructura realizada con piedra, espectadores, hormigón y ese tiempo ritmado.

La combinación de esos elementos acerca la obra a los viejos teatros griegos y el espíritu que debió respirarse en las gradas de Epidauro o Taormina. Incluso la relación con el paisaje y el cierre en tres lados del espectáculo no puede imaginarse muy disímil al de hace dos mil trescientos años en lugares tan lejanos como aquellos anfiteatros griegos. Tampoco puede imaginarse la relación de una masa de personas con un monumento, brutal en su forma y materia, pero cercano a lo exquisito en su concepción, sin enfrentarnos a un conflicto que quizás no estamos preparados para abordar, pero que se pone sobre la mesa en esta obra sin paliativos, ni paños calientes ¿Es posible que uno solo de esos espectadores sumergidos en la multitud sea capaz de salir de esa condición grupal para percatarse de la implacable belleza del lugar en el que se encuentra? ¿Es capaz el estadio, como obra de arquitectura, de golpear con su lógica interna a uno solo de los cerebros que van a vitorear a pleno pulmón a su equipo un domingo por la tarde?

La respuesta se intuye. No obstante, no deja de ser necesario que sea formulada para cualquiera interesado en las posibilidades que la arquitectura tiene de alterar la vida de las personas que la habitan. Es casi seguro que esa misma pregunta ha debido ocupar al autor de esta obra. La distancia entre la forma de la arquitectura propuesta y proyectada, la coherencia y la construcción final, la significación de la obra como ente cultural y el impacto en la vida suponen percibir un abismo difícil de llenar. Ese vacío entre la forma de la arquitectura y la vida creo que es el gran tema que aquí se ofrece actualizado. Y por lo que veo en ella, el aliento que solo alcanzan las obras maestras. Por supuesto que puede analizarse este trabajo en términos más académicos y ortodoxos, y entonces hay que señalar el indudable peso de la monumentalidad piranesiana de las escaleras, el juego de referencia entre la tensión de su cubierta y una tensión hermana a miles de kilómetros, en el aeropuerto Dulles de Chicago, de Eero Saarinen, donde una lámina suspendida con puntales se tensa de un modo extremadamente familiar al de este estadio, y donde la geometría de la catenaria y la contrainclinación de los soportes ayudan a la natural estabilidad del conjunto, como se haría con un tendal.

Igualmente debería hacerse referencia a una obra más cercana en el espacio, y solo ligeramente anterior en el tiempo, de dos renombrados arquitectos portugueses, Álvaro Siza y Eduardo Souto de Moura, quienes, en el pabellón de Lisboa de año 1998, tensaron una sábana semejante creando una plaza en sombra, pero donde los esfuerzos para sostenerla se disimulaban allí entre machones estáticos y serenos, casi italianos...

Pero, ¿importa saber quién es el autor de este crustáceo de hormigón que es el estadio de Braga? Tal vez no.

Decíamos que estamos ante una obra maestra. Sin embargo, no podemos olvidar que, como tipología, las obras maestras requieren de cierta inocencia por parte de sus autores. Por eso, cuando se logra una, el propio concepto de autoría queda desbordado por la obra que de algún modo engulle a su autor. En este sentido, Flaubert se lamentaba de que la vulgar mujerzuela que era Madame Bovary hubiese alcanzado mayor inmortalidad que él mismo. ¿Cómo era posible que un ser ficticio tuviese asegurada la vida y la fama más allá del tiempo? ¿Sucederá igual en este caso del estadio de Braga? ¿Qué piensa de ello su autor? ¿Qué piensa Souto de Moura?

II.

Desde muy temprano, Eduardo Souto de Moura gozó de una atención inhabitual por parte de los especialistas. Las publicaciones de arquitectura se hicieron muy pronto eco de aquel joven colaborador de Álvaro Siza que ya construía independiente una casa desde una ruina, en Gerês, y el prometedor mercado en la ciudad de Braga a principios de los años ochenta, y que mostraba un modo de hacer arquitectura privado de la condición escultórica de su maestro, pero con una sensibilidad hacia la materia y su memoria poco común en el panorama portugués de aquel momento. Con el paso de los años y de las obras, y sumado al reconocimiento profesional, Souto de Moura se ha convertido en un arquitecto extremadamente popular también entre el público no especializado de la arquitectura. Aunque para ello hayan trascurrido más de dos décadas, el hecho de que haya llegado a proyectar la residencia del futbolista más famoso del mundo da fe del inhabitual eco que tiene su trabajo incluso en su propio país. Sin embargo, y dolorosamente para Souto de Moura, esa popularidad se funda en un permanente malentendido, y de ahí precisamente provienen algunas de las incomodidades en las que desarrolla su trabajo. Por este malentendido, sus seguidores han poblado Portugal de cajas elementales al más puro «estilo Souto de Moura» –que él llega a denominar sin atisbo de ironía con el término de «microondas»– y han hecho de su trabajo un territorio susceptible de estar bajo un permanente escrutinio formal a la búsqueda de nuevo material que imitar.

Tal vez a ello contribuya el mundo de la fácil adquisición y difusión de las imágenes en que nos hayamos inmersos, pero lo cierto es que la dificultad de realizar una lectura profunda de su arquitectura por medio de la fotografía ha jugado en contra de la real comprensión de unas obras que parecen fáciles de imitar si no se presta excesiva atención a sus detalles más complejos y sutiles. T. S. Eliot decía al respecto de esa relación del maestro con sus discípulos y la imitación:

> A un discípulo auténtico le causa impresión lo que su maestro dice y, como consecuencia, su manera de decirlo; a un imitador –y podría decir, a uno que copia– le causa impresión principalmente la manera en que lo dijo el maestro. Si consigue parodiar a su maestro suficientemente bien, puede llegar incluso a ocultarse a sí mismo el hecho de que no tiene nada que decir.[1]

Estos problemas, tanto el de ser imitado sin un exceso de hondura como el de ser considerado un maestro, han preocupado a Souto de Moura por diferentes razones.

Por otro lado, el «estilo Souto de Moura» resulta en sí mismo una paradoja, y es que no es fácil clasificar una producción tan heterogénea en los marcos conceptuales en los que se le ha tratado de encasillar. Por Kenneth Frampton, promotor del memorable emparejamiento de regionalismo crítico, ha sido etiquetado como localista. Sin embargo, este concepto apenas sirve para entender el fenómeno portugués en su complejidad y, menos aún, para enmarcar una obra que va más allá de una ambigua «tradición lacónica» ligada a la modernidad. Incluso el hecho de denominar ese contexto en el que Souto de Moura, Álvaro Siza y Fernando Távora han trabajado como Escuela de Oporto ha provocado, tal vez por la mera enunciación, su misma posibilidad. La llamada Escuela de Oporto, de hecho, ha dejado a sus participantes en un territorio en el que ninguno parece sentirse cómodo.

Sin embargo, lo anterior no significa que el papel de la crítica en torno al trabajo de Souto de Moura haya resultado improductivo ni falto de perspicacia. Si bien las vías principales para su análisis han pasado por subrayar todo tipo de continuidades, con la ciudad de Oporto y con Siza y Távora, o por analizar las influencias en su obra de Mies van der Rohe, de Rossi, de la arquitectura popular o del

trabajo de sus colegas más contemporáneos, en última instancia las aproximaciones realizadas por Antonio Esposito y Giovanni Leoni, Nuno Grande y, más recientemente en términos puro-visuales, Juan Antonio Cortés han resultado aún más ajustadas y de mayor alcance, porque han abierto el camino a desentrañar el trabajo de una figura que se resiste a ejercer el incierto papel de maestro, a hablar de estilo e incluso a ser entendido desde un tipo de elementarismo reduccionista.

En cierto modo, Souta de Moura ha permanecido refractario a cada intento de unificar su obra. Ni un arañazo crítico parece haber dejado al descubierto una línea argumental clara en el conjunto de su trabajo. Ni acaso cuando se han tratado de establecer frágiles periodos, conjuntos o familiaridades temáticas, parece que el resultado haya sido plenamente satisfactorio. Los saltos entre sus obras son tales, no solo a nivel proyectual, sino de soluciones y lógicas internas, que la etiqueta de «heteronimia» se queda corta o, cuando menos, manifiesta la confesión de que todo intento de unificación de su trabajo solo cabe bajo el signo de lo imposible de juntar. Y es que en el caso de Souto de Moura existe una real dificultad para penetrar en una coraza conceptual que, sin embargo, no parece voluntaria ni fabricada por él mismo, ni acaso basada en unos presupuestos teóricos inmarcesibles, sino que es el fruto directo del modo en que se forja cada proyecto y de sus concretas circunstancias. Él mismo parece tratar de querer averiguar su auténtica forma de hacer y su propio papel en la arquitectura. Hurga sobre su misma superficie como arquitecto, como lo ha intentado hacer la crítica, aunque empleando el propio proyecto y el acto de proyectar como escarpelo. Dicho de otro modo: en Souto de Moura puede percibirse un esfuerzo suplementario de introspección sobre lo que es la arquitectura y su posición relativa frente a ese objeto hermoso, brillante e inalcanzable en torno al que orbita su actividad. En eso se distancia indudablemente de Siza, para quien esa misma pregunta es ociosa, puesto que la arquitectura no es un fenómeno exterior a sí mismo, o para Távora, para quien la cuestión sobre la arquitectura se responde en cada obra en términos de pura continuidad, como lo hace todo fenómeno de la cultura...

III.

Veinte años separan a Eduardo Souto de Moura de Álvaro Siza. Treinta le alejan, a su vez, de Fernando Távora. La diferencia generacional entre ellos, las propias declaraciones de admiración y familiaridad mutuas, más las recíprocas deudas intelectuales, en absoluto evidentes, bastarían para entender que cualquier intento de simplificar esa cadena dándole el nombre de «escuela» resulta difícilmente operativo. Justificar una sola de las obras de esos arquitectos por su relación con los otros podría descubrir un profundo sistema de vasos comunicantes, pero seguramente se trataría de algo más especulativo que real. El origen de esas mutuas influencias se basa en algo más que en meras intenciones o respeto y proviene de un centro que queda fuera del territorio abarcable por la crítica convencional, ya que roza los terrenos de la psicología o, cuando menos, de la pura hermenéutica.

Con todo, el modo en que estos tres arquitectos tan disímiles han hibridado su trabajo se produce de una forma sumamente extraña en la arquitectura moderna, ya que no solo se da a través de una cadena descendente, sino de un modo recíproco y alternativo, rico e impredecible, saltando edades y momentos a lo largo de los años, con periodos de solape, de cercanía o de alejamiento en los intereses de cada uno de ellos. El mismo Álvaro Siza ha puesto el dedo en la llaga cuando ha reconocido esa deuda no solo con Távora sino, en un sentido bidireccional, con Souto de Moura:

> No tengo ningún reparo en admitir que la influencia fue recíproca, un hecho que quizá nunca se haya analizado a fondo».[2]

Por eso, cuando Fernando Távora habla a su vez del vínculo con Siza y Eduardo Souto de Moura en términos de «casa» común, no solamente lo hace en su sentido literal, por el edificio donde todos compartieron espacio, sino por el modo en que tomó forma de casa esa red de vínculos. Tal vez por eso Távora mismo llegó a denominar también ese espacio compartido y ese tejido de conexiones como una «catedral de la arquitectura», poniendo de manifiesto que las costuras entre ellos rescatan un clima que se aproxima, más bien, al que existía entre los arquitectos medievales y los grandes espacios espirituales del gótico.[3] Entre ellos, efectivamente hay una infiltración intelectual que trasciende el mero traspaso de ideas, formas o rasgos estilísticos, y por eso desborda a los participantes y nos obliga a hacer una pregunta de mayor calado pero de difícil respuesta: ¿cuál es el canal por el que se trasmite la maestría?, ¿cuál es la conexión, la temperatura que subsume la de la mera proximidad física para que la influencia se dé como hecho cierto?

Hace tiempo, Giorgio Grassi dijo respecto a la maestría que la hay de dos tipos: la de los maestros que nos animan, los que nos refuerzan en los momentos de tribulación, los que nos insuflan ánimos y nos acompañan, en fin, la de los maestros «tutelares»; y luego la de los otros, los que nos marcan el rasero de lo que significa la profesión, los que nos dejan en soledad y nos la exigen, los que nos martirizan con esa exigencia y nos impiden caer en la autocomplacencia del trabajo fácil.[4] Grassi olvidaba decir que la maestría genera un ansia moral que tiene una importante cláusula encubierta y que es pertinente no pasar por alto en el caso de Souto de Moura: desafortunadamente, el decirse hijo de un maestro, y hasta su mera proximidad, supone recibir una herencia que puede dejarle a uno sepultado por la carga de la parálisis o la infidelidad. En realidad, ¿cómo esquivar la responsabilidad de esa maestría cercana de Távora y Siza? ¿Dónde buscar un discípulo digno que continúe esa cadena? ¿Y qué supone en el caso de Souto de Moura la actualización contemporánea de la misma palabra maestría en una profesión y en un tiempo donde la arquitectura permanece muy alejada de toda relación gremial como la que implica esa palabra y donde la palabra misma parece haberse entendido como una licencia sin límites para perpetrar cualquier arquitectura? Souto de Moura avanza en una dirección clara en su respuesta cuando pone en valor el anonimato como forma legítima de ejercer su profesión[5] y a la vez se sitúa respecto a Siza y Távora libre de la presión asfixiante de su maestrazgo. (Hasta que, misteriosamente, él mismo produce una obra maestra, claro está.)

De hecho, el caso de estos tres arquitectos sería un laboratorio óptimo para entender, a día de hoy, lo que supone la viralidad real del conocimiento de esta disciplina, antes que para entender la arquitectura de Oporto o sus trabajos individuales. Y aunque las declaraciones de los implicados suelen carecer de importancia, sobre el íntimo funcionamiento de esa cadena nadie ha dicho más y más claramente que el propio Souto de Moura:

> No se trata de un intercambio de influencias arquitectónicas, pero para mí no siempre ha sido así. Creo que he tenido influencias directas, quizá no transposiciones directas, pero si, por ejemplo, tengo que remodelar un edificio antiguo, me resulta muy difícil no hacer referencia a Távora. Si tengo que proyectar una ventana, pienso de manera automática en la casa de Ofir. No se trata de una cuestión de lenguaje o estilo, ni siquiera de método; no me viene a la cabeza la ventana en sí, pero pienso en sus proporciones, en cómo se abre en una pared. Me ocurre lo mismo con Siza. No todo puede ser en ángulo recto, y cuando he proyectado una casa estrecha en una calle donde era imposible mantener los muros rectos, he pensado en Siza, aunque nunca haya construido con curvas. Valoro sus obras una a una y no me dejo prender por su tono, sino que las considero como un Neufert subsconsciente que surge en determinadas circunstancias.[6]

Por otro lado, y si se hace difícil hablar de la obra de Eduardo Souto de Moura según su relación con esos maestros tutelares, tampoco resulta muy tranquilizador hacerlo dentro de la red de influencias marcadas por el contexto meramente físico de Portugal. Adelantando algunas ideas, puede decirse que las propias obras, por sí mismas, dan fe de que hay muchos Soutos de Moura en el arquitecto Eduardo Souto de Moura, o al menos un intento por desdibujar el protagonismo: una voluntad de anonimato y de esquivar todo atisbo de maestría que también se hace por el convencimiento de que hay maneras alternativas de entender el trabajo del arquitecto fuera de la genialidad. Quizás por eso mismo Souto de Moura ha destacado la importancia de los arquitectos de segunda línea cuando ha declarado su admiración por Jorge Segurado, o por Alberto Pessoa, Ruy d'Athouguia y Pedro Cid, autores del edificio de la Sede y Museo Calouste Gulbenkian en Lisboa, entre otros.[7]

Poner el foco sobre esta segunda línea significa dejar de considerar la historia de la arquitectura portuguesa como una mera sucesión de grandes arquitectos y pasar a verla como parte de un conjunto mayor de arquitecturas europeas y occidentales. La nebulosa de obras y arquitectos fuera del foco de la historia es la que construye el panorama en el que se da la pervivencia de las ciudades y también es el sostén del clima, de la atmósfera, en la que realizan sus obras los Siza o Távora de turno, en un ecosistema complejo y nada fácil de simplificar bajo ninguna etiqueta como es la de «escuela».

IV.

Tres familias de esquinas. De ellas, el Mercado de Braga es el símbolo de una primera familia. Pero, ¿qué Mercado de Braga?, ¿el construido por un bisoño Souto de Moura en el año 1977 o el demolido por ese otro Souto de Moura maduro y descreído veinte años después? En realidad no importan las actitudes y los cambios en esos dos arquitectos, ni sus traumas, ni sus alegrías, porque los muros permanecen erguidos frente a cualquier rencilla y ajuste de cuentas. Las esquinas se han defendido de la demolición (no así la cubierta, que ha sido exterminada y convertida en patio y jardín). Las esquinas se mantienen y se prolongan marcando líneas de fuga y clavando el proyecto al suelo. Esos muros se extienden y pesan, y se construyen lejos de la abstracción debido a su fuerte materialidad, aunque al principio exista alguno de ellos que se atreva a flotar (como en la Galería de Arte de Praça de Lisboa o en el interior de la Casa das Artes en Oporto).

De esa familia que no fabrica esquinas sino aristas, forman parte muchas de sus casas de muros de la primera década de su trayectoria profesional, como las casas en Negovilde, las casas patio de Matosinhos (1993-1999) y la Casa das Artes de Oporto (1981-1991). En todas se explora un lenguaje de planos que se desbordan y deslizan desde un ficticio volumen cerrado. En todas ellas, los muros son masivos y, en numerosas ocasiones, contribuyen a la estabilidad del terreno al ser muros que sostienen tierras del otro lado. Cuando el muro llega a su fin, las esquinas son un signo de la construcción, se abren y muestran sus tripas, aunque no con la crudeza con que lo ha hecho en alguna obra Rem Koolhaas, sino con el cuidado de quien enseña ordenadamente las capas de lo constructivo que lo conforman. Souto de Moura dice de esas esquinas y del porqué mostrar sus planos superpuestos: «Un único muro de piedra de 20 cm de grosor no puede responder al diferente comportamiento de los materiales en el exterior, en el interior, en la piel y en la estructura. Todavía queda por resolver el maldito puente térmico, que nos obliga a mentir y cambiar continuamente».[8]

Frente a la esquina de un muro de Mies, las de Souto de Moura no tratan de fingir un grosor puro, sino que aceptan el juego de su complejidad. No es posible dejar de lado el modo en que Mies y Souto de Moura se enfrentan al remate de esas aristas: el primero, con una pieza masiva del mismo material, y pienso por ejemplo en los muros de ónice del Pabellón de Barcelona; el otro, con una exfoliación de sus capas. El complejo primitivismo de dejar esa arista a la vista de sus grosores reales está a medio camino entre lo delicado y el modo en que resolvería esa especialización del muro la arquitectura anónima y popular. En cierto sentido, hace parecer a uno mucho anterior al otro. De hecho, ¿sería posible que Souto de Moura fuese un antecedente de Mies van der Rohe? A veces, la poesía es más real que la historia: la Casa de Ladrillo de Mies indudablemente copia a Eduardo Souto de Moura y supone un avance en el modo en que sus muros se han liberado de la necesidad de contener tierras. Y si esto resulta tan verosímil es porque, de algún secreto modo, la obra de Souto de Moura ha alterado la lectura que hacemos de Mies van der Rohe: desde Souto de Moura percibimos en Mies una faceta mucho más impura y compleja del arquitecto alemán, algo que se produce más allá de lo detectado por Rowe en aquella esquina que recubría la estructura con perfiles de bronce en el edificio Seagram.

Este juego de la disolución de la temporalidad es uno de los problemas centrales a la hora de interpretar el trabajo de Souto de Moura. Parece arrancar precisamente de un punto donde lo moderno está por definir o ha sido completamente superado, de un punto donde la modernidad está en discusión, sea por primitivismo o por posmodernidad.

La segunda familia de esquinas la podemos encontrar en el edificio de la Rua do Teatro, un edificio de apartamentos que se dirige con todo su ser al frente de la calle, aunque lo haga por medio del acomodo de volúmenes de distintos tamaños. La trama de acero que recubre la fachada es una piel uniforme

y sofisticada, con perfiles de acero de igual dimensión que, pese a ello, logran disimular los espesores constructivos reales de los forjados del suelo, las paredes y la cubierta que tapan. Este no es un detalle menor para entender el tipo de estrategias que le gusta emplear a Souto de Moura, y es que no hay una manera sencilla de hacer que una cubierta posea el mismo espesor que un forjado de una planta intermedia, al menos en el contexto tecnológico y cultural de la construcción en Portugal, porque deben resolverse en ese punto los aislamientos y los problemas de estanqueidad del edificio, y resulta obvio que no ocupan el mismo espacio.

Además, la trama de acero en fachada prioriza, con el sentido de colocación de su perfil, una dirección, haciendo del frente a la calle el alzado principal. El mismo detalle de cada una de las uniones entre perfiles horizontales y verticales manifiesta una narrativa de «frente y laterales» y de orden constructivo en la que se remarca el protagonismo de la arista.

Como decíamos, los perfiles en H, perfiles de sombra, se disparan en una sola dirección; a ese gesto se somete la totalidad de la obra. Tanto es así que cualquiera que se tome el tiempo que merece observar las plantas verá que hasta las mismas particiones interiores, a pesar de su aparente soltura y libertad, se redireccionan y corrigen en el último instante para llegar contra esa trama de acero sin hacerle modificar su trazado. Mientras, los laterales de esas cajas se convierten en puras fachadas secundarias, recubriéndose de pizarra o sin siquiera abrir huecos en ellas.

Esos volúmenes, cuidadosos con la escala en relación al barrio, permanecen puros, sin roturas ni gestos estridentes en su contorno, con ese aire norteamericano de los edificios proyectados por SOM en los años sesenta. Su lenguaje puede ser entendido dentro de la lógica de una modernidad canónica en relación a la estructura. Sin embargo, dentro siguen una ley compositiva algo anómala y que en absoluto parecería coherente con esa malla de acero que forma cajas esquinadas. Souto de Moura es consciente de lo extraño de esta situación en la que parece como si esa familia de formas de sus primeras casas de muros se hubiese recubierto por una carcasa modulada:

> para proyectar el interior en detalle he seguido un método muy parecido al definido como neoplástico. [...] Esta atmósfera neoplástica de los apartamentos no responde a mi adhesión poética al neoplasticismo, sino a la posibilidad de utilizar conscientemente el método de los arquitectos neoplásticos para subdividir y recomponer los espacios en función de las distintas situaciones a resolver.[9]

Para entender la dificultad de cualquier relación del edificio de la Rua do Teatro con lo neoplástico –y que, sin embargo, sí se podría haber sostenido en los casos de muros que se extienden de la primera familia de esquinas–, tal vez convenga recordar ahora que la meta principal de la vieja poética neoplasticista se concentraba en la disolución de la caja como artificio compositivo. La arquitectura de Frank Lloyd Wright, desde la Casa Robie a las Usonian y Prairie Houses, y la de todo Mies van der Rohe, se fundaron sobre la simpleza de un descubrimiento que ponía el foco en las esquinas de la arquitectura. Reventada la caja, libre de sus ataduras portantes, los planos de sus caras no eran más que objetos abstractos. Basta recordar la Casa Schröder en Utrecht de Gerrit Rietveld, por ejemplo, para entender cómo el despliegue de la caja en el espacio implicaba el intento de disolución de todo límite posible, incluso la diferencia entre interior y exterior. Desde ese instante, la preeminencia de un discurso basado en toda dialéctica de fachadas principales y secundarias pasó a ser, en apariencia, de segundo orden, y el discurso de lo material basculó hacia lo abstracto, llenándose las paredes de colores planos y sin peso.

Sin embargo, y si ya hemos visto la predilección por la materia en los muros neoplásticos de Souto de Moura, en esta obra, la lógica de la descomposición de planos está ya muy debilitada, tanto que ni siquiera posee la musculatura para deshacer las esquinas de esas cajas bien formadas. Las aristas no están aquí libres de la responsabilidad de sustentar el peso de la obra, sino más bien sucede todo lo contrario: se subrayan con líneas dibujadas con acero. Esta contradicción flagrante entre una caja y su interior neoplástico no dejaría tranquilo a ningún espíritu moderno. Por eso, ¿qué tipo de juego conceptual permite a un edificio disfrutar de sistemas compositivos a voluntad sin romper el presupuesto de la coherencia? Solo se me ocurre contestar que se trata de una lógica amparada bajo un cierto descreimiento posmoderno. O bajo el espíritu de un auténtico *bricoleur*...

En esta problemática donde solo la materia en su detalle intenta prolongarse, podríamos añadir los casos como el de la torre de oficinas Burgo. En esas esquinas, donde las franjas de fachada se separan o solapan mostrando el alternante ritmo del apilamiento, resuenan el modo en que se acumulan los troncos en los secaderos de madera y hasta los juegos de piezas infantiles. No obstante, a su vez, allí se vuelven sutiles ejercicios de construcción y de escala. Desde la lectura de su esquina es posible determinar cuál es nuevamente la fachada que se impone, pero tan solamente por la leve sugerencia que se ofrece al mostrarse el canto de una materia que es más ligera y de menor grosor que lo que cabría esperar para el granito, pero que se asoma y se extiende como planos sin peso en cada pieza: una esquina como miniatura neoplástica a escala dos a uno.

Una tercera familia de esquinas tiene que ver con la rotura del volumen en sus aristas. En esos puntos, la caja se vacía o se interseca con volúmenes colocados en las aristas, como en la Casa do Cinema de Manoel de Oliveira. En todo caso, el vacío en esos puntos trastoca el sentido del peso que tiene toda caja opaca y masiva, convirtiendo el volumen en un juego cercano a lo escultórico, pero donde todo se aligera y se vuelve más etéreo y liviano.

La sistematización de ese lenguaje de esquinas ausentes es notable en el Museo Paula Rêgo. En las salas, por el mero abrirse en esos puntos se deshace además el previsible sistema de recorridos que todo museo desea para facilitar la lógica expositiva. Cada sala se abre al exterior o a otras salas en sus esquinas rotas, pero lo hace reduciendo la escala precisamente en los puntos de transición. El carácter singular de esos «pasos rotos» es siempre puerta o ventana, escalón o nicho, punto singular. La pérdida de un lenguaje reconocible y su anonimato suponen un inquietante salto cualitativo en su trabajo. En ellas ya no está un Souto de Moura reconocible, sino que asoman otro tipo de influencias. Y de oportunidades.

Este mismo problema de las esquinas que muerden un volumen no significa que deba ser exclusivamente tratado en el plano de las aristas verticales, sino que el vaciado puede darse también con el plano del suelo, como sucede con el museo de Arte Contemporáneo de Braganza, donde el contacto se vuelve un lugar de juego con el peso del propio edificio.

El conjunto de estas tres familias de esquinas sería suficiente para señalar cuánto nos encontramos hablando de una arquitectura que debe ser tratada y entendida en términos de puro lenguaje y de su sintaxis. En la arquitectura de Souto de Moura, el hecho de entender el carácter de la arquitectura como un ordenado conjunto de formas capaces de construir un sentido puede entenderse también por medio de la aproximación que ofrecen las referencias empleadas.[10]

V.

Souto de Moura es un *collagista* ejemplar, un recolector excepcional de objetos de arquitectura que sabiamente quedan dispuestos en la obra. Sin embargo, los bordes de esos objetos han sido cuidadosamente rehabilitados en su segundo uso para borrar sus fronteras. Cada objeto, cada cita y cada préstamo ha sido pulido cuidadosamente. No hay grumos de pegamento o toscas soldaduras como sucedería en los primitivos colajes tridimensionales de Picasso o de Schwitters. El mundo de los *objets trouvés* en Souto de Moura es un mundo sin polvo ni suciedad. He ahí su mayor problema interpretativo. Sus obras son colajes que se dan sin conflicto visible. Permanecen camuflados de elementarismo, salvo en un punto donde ninguna obra de colaje es capaz de disimular: en las esquinas.

¿Qué es el Pabellón de Viana do Castelo si se priva del juego de las instalaciones a modo de sombrero que lo coronan como los laureles de los antiguos atletas olímpicos? ¿O sin mantener en la memoria la inevitable referencia al Museo Pompidou? ¿Qué es el Estadio de Braga sino un gran teatro griego? ¿Qué son la rehabilitación de Santa María do Bouro o el metro de Oporto sino obras sin autor, infraestructurales, donde el *bricoleur* ha logrado camuflarse en el anonimato, donde el arquitecto se esconde en una trabajada segunda fila?

El colaje es empleado sistemáticamente por Souto de Moura, pero si es tan difícil de detectar es porque, al contrario de lo que cabría esperar, existe en su trabajo un esfuerzo descomunal por disolver los conflictos y los bordes, por atenuar las contradicciones y hasta hacer desaparecer al autor.

A este respecto, se ha prestado poca atención crítica a un texto que resulta trascendente para entender su modo de hacer a pesar de su brevedad: *Nexus*. Está compuesto de fragmentos al más puro estilo de Benjamin y, en él, su interés por un método cercano al del montaje cinematográfico es evidente: «reescribo como en un colaje, son palabras de otros que he hecho mías: de algunos no conozco siquiera el nombre. Es como un reflejo condicionado, un vértigo sobre el papel».[11]

Lo importante del colaje para Souto de Moura es que con él desaparecían algunas de las necesidades y traumas de la modernidad. Con él, es posible decir cosas nuevas con cosas usadas. Con él, el autor no se ve impelido a crear con el peso y la maldición de hacerlo desde cero, sino a reacoplar mejor las piezas existentes. El colaje es operativo para Souto de Moura porque le permite rellenar el monstruoso hueco que hay entre la arquitectura y la vida. Precisamente entre el mundo del edificio y el mundo de los habitantes existe un campo que ha sido pasado por alto pero que a Souto de Moura le interesa, porque en él percibe el trauma moderno y posmoderno en que se encuentra la arquitectura contemporánea. Ese campo intermedio es un espacio fértil para el malentendido, pero también para los errores y las encrucijadas. Es el espacio entre lo previsto por el proyecto y lo que realmente ocurre con la arquitectura al ser vivida.

El siglo XX nos permitió ver el colaje como un modo de hacer libre de la academia y de la especialización. El bricolaje no exigía teorías, ni unos sofisticados conocimientos previos. Hoy sabemos que el colaje es el medio más certero para describir el modo de apropiación de la arquitectura por parte de los habitantes. Para Souto de Moura el colaje supone la plena y liberadora consciencia de lo poco que un arquitecto sabe, de lo poco que controla la forma hasta sus últimas consecuencias. Souto de Moura nos descubre que la arquitectura recibe su sentido de la vida y no de su autor. Puede que esa consciencia sea el centro constitutivo de su maestría.

1. T. S. Eliot: *Criticar al crítico* [Madrid: Alianza Editorial], 1957, 69. Traducción de M. Rivas Corral.
2. Antonio Esposito y Giovanni Leoni: «Fernando Távora. Álvaro Siza y Eduardo Souto de Moura, una conversación», en *Eduardo Souto de Moura* [Barcelona: Gustavo Gili], 2003, 11.
3. Antonio Esposito y Giovanni Leoni: «Fernando Távora. Álvaro Siza y Eduardo Souto de Moura, una conversación», *op. cit.* 15.
4. Giorgio Grassi: «Antiguos maestros», en *Arquitectura lengua muerta y otros escritos* [Barcelona: Ediciones del Serbal], 2003. Traducción de R. Mora, M. Iñíguez, A. Ustárroz, J. L Aristu.
5. 'En cuanto a mí, es evidente que mi ambición es quedar codificado, resultar anónimo, porque cuando uno queda codificado se vuelve anónimo'. En Nuno Grande: «Regreso a casa: una conversación con Eduardo Souto de Moura», en *El Croquis n.º 146, Souto de Moura, 2005-2009, Teatros del mundo*, 2009, 23.
6. Antonio Esposito y Giovanni Leoni: «Fernando Távora, Álvaro Siza y Eduardo Souto de Moura: una conversación», *op. cit.* 15.
7. José Morales: «Domesticar la arquitectura: una conversación con Eduardo Souto de Moura», en *El croquis n.º 176, Eduardo Souto de Moura 2009-2014*, 2015, 6 y ss.
8. Antonio Esposito y Giovanni Leoni: «Nexus», *op. cit.* 363-367.
9. Antonio Esposito y Giovanni Leoni: «Edificios en bloque», *op. cit.* 215.
10. En el Museo Paula Rego, por ejemplo, el peso de Rossi, de las citas a Siza o al arquitecto local Raul Lino son declaradas y hacen de la obra un sumatorio de *objets trouvés*.
11. Antonio Esposito y Giovanni Leoni: «Nexus», *op. cit.* 364.

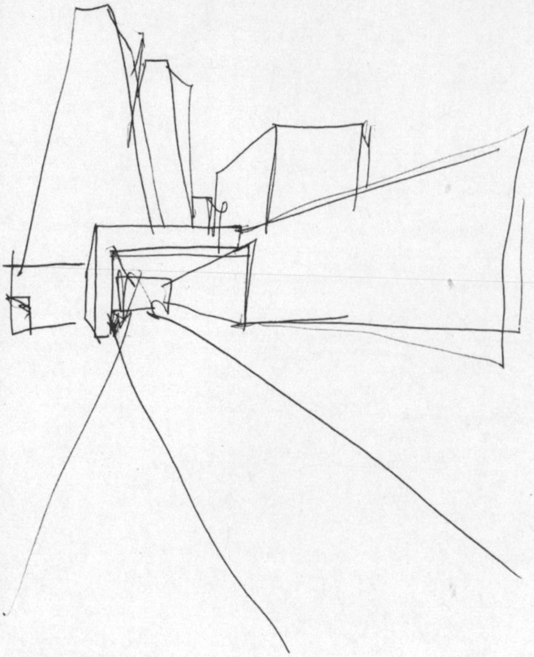